ALLEN RIDER GUIDES

ALLEN RIDER GUIDES

RIDING FROM SCRATCH

RIDING FROM SCRATCH

MARTIN DIGGLE

J. A. ALLEN · LONDON

British Library Cataloguing in Publication Data
A catalogue record for this book is available from the British Library.

ISBN 0. 85131. 682.4

© Diggle, Martin

First published in 1987 by J. A. Allen and Co. Ltd.
Revised edition 1997

Published in Great Britain in 1997 by
J. A. Allen & Company Limited,
1, Lower Grosvenor Place, Buckingham Palace Road,
London, SW1W 0EL

Design and typesetting by Paul Saunders
Photographs by L.E. Raper-Zullig and Iain Burns
Cartoons by Ann Pilgrim
Line illustrations by Rodney Paull

Printed in Hong Kong by Dah Hua Printing Press Co.

CONTENTS

7 OTHER ASPECTS OF LEARNING

CONCLUSION

PREFACE

A friend of mine had a greengrocery shop, a young family and a certain talent for karate. One day, he decided to take up riding. Some years later, he had become the proprietor and chief instructor of a large equestrian centre. His own mare, purchased as an unbroken three-year-old, became an Intermediate eventer, and won a class at the Horse of the Year Show. His son and daughter, taught largely by their father, have become highly successful competitors and trainers in the sports of showjumping and dressage.

Admittedly, my friend's talent and enthusiasm for riding turned out to be much above average – but he didn't know that when he went for his first ride.

A main purpose of this book is to persuade newcomers to riding that they do not have to settle for the status of permanent novices so, although I do not claim that anyone can match my friend's achievements, I cite him as an example of what is possible if one does not put a false ceiling upon one's ambitions.

INTRODUCTION

Until well into the first part of the twentieth century horses, ridden or driven, were a very common form of transport. Although their use purely for sporting purposes was mainly the province of wealthier members of society, many other people rode, drove or handled them as part of everyday life, and many farmers and tradesmen rode and hunted their utility ride-and-drive cobs.

With the advent and development of motor vehicles however, this state of affairs underwent radical change and, within a few decades, the working horse was superceded to a large degree by various forms of mechanised transport.

During the transitional period there was some shift of emphasis towards riding for pleasure on the part of 'ordinary' people, the main motivating bodies being the Institute of the Horse and the National Horse Association. The Pony and Riding Club movements were established (some clubs being based on workplace), and a number of riding schools sprang up catering for clients across the social spectrum. Riding was, in fact, on the way to becoming a popular (if still minority) sport when the Second World War intervened.

During the war years, enthusiasts made extraordinary efforts to keep their horses, a number of charity shows were organised, and the demands of the times revived and prolonged the use of horse-drawn transport. However, riding for pleasure was scarcely a priority during this period, and the overall effect of the war and its aftermath on riding was distinctly negative. This resulted from various factors; in addition to personal tragedies and hardship a number of urban schools had been reduced to rubble, and priorities of land use and increased costs prevented their reinstatement. Also, the renewed acceleration in the development and use of mechanised transport once more distracted attention from the horse and, as a result of these influences, a post-war generation grew up in which, for the first time in centuries, a large proportion of the population had no real knowledge of the horse.

It was against this unpromising background that riding began to re-emerge as an increasingly popular sport. There was a combination of reasons for this: firstly, the general austerity of the post-war era began to ease, leaving many people with rather more money and leisure time, and a growing desire to enjoy themselves once more. Secondly, the war itself had erased any last vestiges of interest in cavalry as a practical fighting force, and a number of military riding instructors opened new commercial schools upon leaving the army. Thirdly, in these years, Britain enjoyed a great deal of success in international riding competitions, and this coincided with the emergence of a number of outstanding 'characters', both equine and human. Public interest was thus stimulated, especially as the increasingly popular and influential medium of television brought showjumping in particular to an ever-widening audience. Furthermore, at this time, the organisation and promotion of shows and riding was in the hands of a group of people who not only had a great deal of equestrian knowledge, but also a high degree of administrative ability, and they both recognised and encouraged the increasing interest. These factors, combined with a generally retained affection for the horse, led to a growth in the popularity of riding which continues to the present time at an accelerating rate.

However, the fact that so many people nowadays come into riding with no background knowledge of 'what makes horses tick', and only the vaguest notion of what they, personally, can expect from the sport, creates a distinctly two-edged situation. One the one hand, given sound instruction and encouragement, they may get more from riding than they would think possible. On the other hand, if they receive inadequate, bad or dangerous instruction (which is, unfortunately, by no means out of the question), they may end up disillusioned or even injured. This book, therefore, attempts not only to explain the basic principles and techniques of riding, but also to help the reader discern the differences between good and bad tuition and appreciate the opportunities which may exist once the basics are learnt.

— 1 —

GETTING STARTED

■ Learning to Ride Correctly

There are many and various reasons why people actually decide to take up riding: a general affinity toward horses; a feeling that it 'might be fun'; desire for more exercise; influence of family or friends, and so on.

One point common to many beginners, however, is that they have little idea of what they would actually like to achieve in

Learning to ride is fun!

riding, and, consequently, no real goals. This is not really surprising, since riding differs in many ways from most other sports, especially the more popular ball and team games. One could, for instance, take lessons in squash with the definite aim of climbing as far as possible up the club 'ladder', or perhaps nurture a cricketing ambition of being a seam bowler or a wicketkeeper. With riding, however, few people visualise themselves initially as a showjumper or dressage exponent. This may be because their only experience of such sports has been through watching international competitions on television, and they assume that such activities are the exclusive province of the rich and brilliant. Whatever the reason, the fact remains that most people start off with the idea that they would 'just like to be good enough to ride a bit', which can usually be construed as being capable of going hacking (riding out sedately – hopefully under escort).

Now there is nothing wrong with hacking, and there are many people who do 'learn to ride a bit', and go on to enjoy seeing the countryside from horseback. For these people, however, riding remains a recreation rather than a sport, and it is my contention that they are missing an awful lot of the fun, excitement and challenge that riding can offer, and they may also be putting themselves at greater risk than necessary. Let us consider these contentions in more detail, since the thoughts behind them may give the newcomer a better idea of what riding is all about.

The fun, excitement and challenge of riding are heightened by an interest in the specific sports which can be pursued on horseback. It is not only the household names who participate in dressage, showjumping and horse trials ('eventing'); these sports can be enjoyed at an appropriate level by anyone who has attained a modest degree of proficiency. Furthermore, many other activities become accessible to the competent rider – hunter trials, hunting, mock hunting, obstacle rides, showing and riding classes to name but some.

A reasonable standard of riding 'on the flat' is an essential pre-

Mark Todd on Horton Point jumping into The Lake at Badminton in 1994.

liminary requirement for any branch of equitation, but, since it is a common basis, progress in any particular sphere is largely a result of building the appropriate skill and knowledge upon that base. Furthermore, the skills and techniques required for various types of riding may well prove complementary to each other, with a skill initially nurtured in pursuit of one particular discipline proving to be beneficial in other circumstances.

Actual participation in sports and competitions is not the only source of enjoyment to be derived from their pursuit. There is, to my mind at least, more satisfaction to be gained from riding a horse for a specific purpose (getting him fit, improving both horse and rider, etc.) than from merely 'going for a ride'. Furthermore, the background work, practice and preparation necessary are major parts of the learning process.

> The various equestrian sports are less mutually exclusive than many people think and, in order to be good at any particular sport, it is first necessary to be good *rider*.

Stimulation is, of course, a key factor in any form of learning, and riding is no exception. Therefore, the rider who has definite aims and aspirations is likely to improve more quickly than the rider who has none, and, as with most activities, increased proficiency will lead to a greater capacity for enjoyment. This enjoyment may take many forms, but a major advantage gained by the proficient rider will be an ability to ride a greater variety of horses to good effect and in safety, and to deal with most difficulties which may arise. This is why I maintain that riders with little or no ambition to improve may be putting themselves at risk, especially if they ride on a casual basis at a variety of different stables. Such risk arises not only from a lower degree of technical ability but also (perhaps more so) from a lack of understanding of equine behaviour, and these factors may sometimes be linked to a lack of interest in, or knowledge of, the horse's soundness and fitness, and the condition and suitability of the saddlery.

Although I do not wish to convey the impression that riding is inherently dangerous, it is a sport which will always contain an element of risk. However, it seems that the majority of accidents which occur do not result from the 'natural risk' element so much as from circumstances which could have been avoided given adherence to correct and safe practices. Therefore, even if you are currently convinced that you do not have any particular equestrian ambitions, I would urge you to get a good basic grounding at a reputable riding school before venturing out on treks or holidays at 'unknown' centres.

However, it is my experience that a significant proportion of riders who start out along such lines soon 'get the bug', and decide that they would, after all, like to try all sorts of equestrian activities. I suggest, therefore, that you keep an open mind in the early stages – you may well surprise yourself.

Keep an open mind. Learning to ride can open up a whole new world!

Finally on this theme, although it is my purpose to encourage as many people as possible to ride for both sport and pleasure, I have a brief message for anyone who might think that riding is just a matter of dressing up in jeans and cowboy boots, hiring a horse and going for a gallop – forget it. Beginners riding unaccompanied are in considerable danger, and only a thoroughly disreputable stable will allow such a practice. Ignoring this advice is not brave or intrepid: it is plain foolishness, and I have known people who have discovered the truth of this the hard way.

▪ The Cost

Riding is generally considered to be an expensive sport, and there is some truth in this assumption. However, for the 'weekend' rider, it is almost certainly less expensive than is popularly imagined, and cost comparisons with other sports would prove more favourable than might be expected. For example, as a golfer as well as a rider, I would suggest that a weekly riding lesson will cost about the same as a round of golf, and the initial capital expenditure on riding equipment will be very much less than the sum which the newcomer to golf might expect to spend. Although I have no costings to back up the supposition, I would imagine that 'growth' sports such as skiing, water-skiing and clay pigeon shooting would all be at least as expensive as riding, and that even angling, pursued on a serious, regular basis, would run it close.

To come down to actual figures (1996 prices), the basic clothing for riding can be bought for around £120, but it is not essential to buy it all at once or, with the exception of a hard hat, even new. The cost of a one hour lesson will be around £15 to £20 and it must be borne in mind that this includes hire of horse, use of facilities and tuition.

In order to maintain reasonable progress it will be necessary to have one weekly lesson, and if you can afford to ride more frequently, so much the better. It is here, in fact, that riding can become costly; many people, having started on the basis of one lesson a week, become so enthusiastic that they begin to want more and, at a later stage, to ride out as well. Riding can become an addiction, but at least it is healthier than most others!

▪ Basic Equipment

The items listed below are necessary from the point of view of safety, efficiency and comfort. While it is not essential that they are all acquired at the outset, there are definite advantages to be gained by obtaining them as soon as possible, as will become apparent with experience.

HARD HAT Protective headgear is essential for the rider, and all reputable riding schools will insist upon its use. Many schools, in fact, keep a supply of hats for loan to pupils, but the safety principle is often partly negated because the hats are in poor condition, of obsolete design or just do not fit the individual. To be fair to the schools, they are not charities, and to maintain a full range of suitable headgear for clients use would cost a considerable sum of money (which would doubtless be reflected in increased prices, or in hire charges), and carry the attendant risk that the hats go missing in unscrupulous hands.

The best way to avoid problems or injury is to purchase a brand new hat of your own, and this should certainly be the first priority as far as equipment is concerned. The British Standard which may currently be considered the 'norm' is BS4472. This was originally developed with reference to race-riding, and BS4472 hats are sometimes referred to as 'crash hats' or 'jockey skulls', although not all BS4472 hats are obviously of this external pattern. Hats conforming to BS4472 are now obligatory wear for many cross-country competitions, and some organisations, such as the Pony Club, insist that BS4472 headgear be worn at all their mounted events.

Research aimed at improving head protection continues on

Skullcap with safety harness worn with a silk cover.

an international basis, and it seems likely that new patterns of headgear, and revised British and International Standards will be introduced in due course. For the moment, the important thing is to buy a hat which conforms to existing Standards, and to avoid anything else. The purchase should be made from a reputable riding outfitters, where the staff will be able to advise on the various important aspects of fitting. Current cost will be in the region of £30–£35, which is pretty cheap considering the protection given, and which will suddenly seem extremely cheap should you have the misfortune to receive a heavy blow on the head. If the hat does ever suffer a heavy impact, it should be discarded (not given to someone else) even if there is no obvious damage. However, in normal use, these hats will last for a number of years.

JODHPURS/ BREECHES Although there are historical and sartorial differences between the two, these are both basically, specially designed riding trousers. They are not essential for first lessons, but they are much more comfortable than the alternatives, and are therefore usually acquired at an early stage.

Jodhpurs worn with a waterproof yard boot.

The main alternatives are jeans and cords, but both tend to ride up on the insides of the knees, and pinch and chafe. Also, the normally rather tight cut of jeans tend to make sitting astride a horse in them a rather hazardous and uncomfortable business. Classical showing or competition jodhpurs/breeches can cost up to £70 or £80, but they can often be picked up for much less in the New Year sales of major outfitters. For general riding, however, there are now ranges of coloured jopdhpurs and breeches on the market, including some made of stretch denim. These are less obtrusive, significantly cheaper than the classical style and may be a practical first buy.

Whatever type you choose, remember when buying them to check that they remain comfortable when you adopt a riding posture.

BOOTS Again, these are not essential for first lessons: a robust pair of walking shoes will suffice. However, plimsolls, trainers, fashion shoes and high heels are dangerous, since they can easily get caught in the stirrups, and provide very little protection if a horse treads on your foot, or even from the stirrup irons bruising the soles of your feet. No instructor who has your welfare at heart will let you ride in such footwear.

Traditional wellingtons are also rather unsatisfactory because, depending upon actual design, there may be a risk that they, too, could get caught in the stirrups. Furthermore, their short leg and loose fit may result in either the rider's legs or the horse's sides being pinched, and the tops of the boots may snag against the panel of the saddle.

Proper riding boots not only avoid potential problems with the stirrups but also provide protection and support for the lower leg. In this latter respect, they have an advantage over both 'dealer' and jodhpur boots, which are only ankle length, and also over the increasingly popular 'muckers'.

Boots, jodhpurs and breeches are available in a wide range of colours and materials.

Rubber boots, traditionally cold in winter and sweaty in summer, are becoming more sophisticated; the better makes having hi-tech linings and good styling. They also have the advantages of being fully waterproof, rot-proof, and easy to clean. It is possible to buy cheap, unlined boots for a few pounds, but you should get much more comfort and wear if you can afford between £30 and £40.

Good leather boots, provided they fit properly and once broken in, are more comfortable than rubber, and should last for years. However, they need a good deal of looking after, and are much too expensive for most people to contemplate as a first purchase. Nevertheless, they can sometimes be picked up secondhand at a favourable price, in which case, as long as they do fit correctly, they are likely to be represent a good buy.

With an eye to winter, it is important to choose boots which are sufficiently roomy to accommodate either two pairs of socks or one pair of very thick thermal ones. Although it contradicts the principles of cold weather clothing, my own preference is for

Long leather boots look marvellous and last for many years.

one thick pair of socks, since two layers tend to restrict movement in the foot, and may induce cramp, which is no fun on horseback.

GLOVES Most people ride for most of the time without gloves, but they can prove very useful indeed. Apart from keeping the hands warm in cold weather, they provide protection from poorly maintained reins and horses who 'pull', and they prevent grazes which could occur in the event of a fall. They are also essential when riding with plain leather reins in wet weather, and on horses who sweat up.

Although some of these uses relate more to the experienced rider, it is likely that everyone will benefit from wearing them sooner or later, and, bearing their various functions in mind, it is worth buying a pair of purpose-made, leather-palmed riding gloves. (If money is tight, synthetic, 'pimple-palm' gloves can be bought very cheaply.)

If you are one of those people who are forever losing *one* glove, there are now some very cheap rubber-palmed gloves available, which are quite serviceable for everyday use.

WHIP Many novice riders feel that it is prentious to carry a whip, and that is clutters their hands up. However, as we shall see in due course, the riding whip is not necessarily (or even primarily) and instrument of punishment, but can be a useful and quite subtle adjunct to the rider's natural aids (signals). It can also be used in exercises to provide a graphic illustration of the stillness or otherwise of the rider's hands.

It is, therefore, well worth obtaining a whip at an early stage and getting used to handling it. There is no need to buy anything elaborate, but you should avoid the cheap, short plastic 'toys', which look like a stick of liquorice and are considerably

This rider is wearing a velvet safety hat with chin strap, and carrying a practical whip of standard length.

less useful. The standard type of whip will be about 75 cm (30 in) long, and cost a few pounds, and I would suggest that this type will be more appropriate for a novice rider than the much longer schooling whip.

A schooling whip, normally 1 m (39 in) or more in length, is intended specifically as a supplementary aid to the rider's leg, and is used with the whip hand still holding the rein. It can be most useful to an experienced rider schooling a horse, but it is unlikely that a novice rider will appreciate properly how and when to apply one, and they may not have developed sufficient co-ordination and control of the hand to do so without interfering with the rein contact on the horse's mouth.

Furthermore, schooling whips are initially more difficult to switch from hand to hand and, looking ahead, they are of limited value when jumping, and exceed the length permitted for whips in many forms of competition.

■ **Finding Somewhere to Learn**

We have seen that riding is a sport which involves an element of risk, and it requires an understanding of how to handle a large, strong animal in a safe and effective manner. It is essential, therefore, that the beginner finds a source of correct instruction. *It is foolish and dangerous in the extreme for a person with little or no knowledge to obtain their own horse and attempt to teach themselves.* Similarly, you should be very wary of being taught by a friend or relative unless they are a professionally qualified instructor, or else a very experienced rider with teaching skills.

Most people learn to ride at a commercial riding school, and these are quite prolific, especially in the outer suburbs of large towns. Unfortunately, standards vary alarmingly and the beginner, operating alone, may be at a considerable disadvantage when it comes to discerning good and bad practices. The situation is further complicated because, while there are some schools which are good in all respects, and some which are so obviously ghastly that their survival defies belief, the majority are something of a mixture. For instance, a school may employ one very able, and one barely competent, instructor, or have high quality horses but poor standards of safety, or have a very good instructor struggling to work with poor quality horses. The permutations are virtually endless but, while this presents a complicated and daunting picture, it should be borne in mind that progress, especially in the early stages, will be very largely dependent upon the tuition received. It is, therefore, well worth making every effort to discover the best school available to you. It is, of course, entirely possible that an experienced friend may be able to recommend a suitable establishment but, if this is not the case, there are several factors which can assist you in making a good choice. These are:

STATUS By status, I mean the school's standing as a legitimate centre for riding instruction. The most fundamental guideline here is that it must hold a licence issued by the relevant local authority under the terms of the 1970 *Riding Establishments Act.* This Act makes it a legal requirement that any stable hiring out horses for general riding, or in connection with instruction for financial reward, must be licenced annually, subject to satisfying the requirements of an inspection.

A list of licenced establishments within their jurisdiction should, therefore, be obtainable from any local authority, and the rider seeking instruction should steer clear of any stables which are unlicenced.

The main concerns of the *Riding Establishments Act* are the general welfare of the horses, public health considerations, fire precautions and the safety of clients insofar as it stipulates the use of saddlery in good condition and the supervision of rides by a person of at least 16 years-of-age. These safety requirements, although of value, do not offer any guarantee that instruction will be of a good (or even safe) standard. Furthermore, whilst the inspectors have to be satisfied that the proprietor or manager of the establishment is suitably experienced this, again, is no intrinsic guarantee of teaching standards.

Therefore, although a list of licenced schools provides a starting point when seeking a place to ride, it is advisable to look for further indications of suitability. In this respect, there are two organisations which will carry out annual inspections of licenced stables for their own 'approval', and these are the British Horse Society (B.H.S.) and the Association of British Riding Schools (A.B.R.S.).

The B.H.S. is the body which administers and promotes riding as a sport and recreation in Britain. The A.B.R.S. is basically a trade association of riding school proprietors. There is no legal requirement for a riding school to be inspected by, or even involved with, either of these bodies, and their jurisdiction (except in respect of being able to report any breaches of the Act to the statutory authority) is limited to the terms of their constitutions. However, it is generally considered that approval by the B.H.S. and/or membership of the A.B.R.S. indicate reasonable standards in a school, and many, therefore, seek such status in their own interests. Although each body places slightly different emphasis upon requirements, inspection by either will reiterate the main points of the Riding Establishments Act, and also place a great emphasis upon teaching standards.

A school approved by the B.H.S. will display a blue plaque to that effect, showing the year of approval (which should be current), and will also be included in literature relating to approved establishments which is available from the B.H.S. bookshop at

The B.H.S. and A.B.R.S. signs displayed by approved riding schools.

The National Equestrian Centre, Stoneleigh, Kenilworth, Warwickshire. A school which has passed the A.B.R.S. inspection will have an 'A.B.R.S. Member' sign on display.

One difficulty with any system of annual inspection is that there is always the possibility that standards are either raised short-term, or else allowed to deteriorate once the inspection has been completed. Riding schools are no exception, and they are complex places to run, being dependent upon many factors and influences for their success or otherwise. It would not be unrealistic to say that there are occasions when a school is found to hold a current licence, or even non-statutory approvals, without apparently meriting such status. Furthermore, neither licences nor approvals are conditional upon, or proof of, all-round excellence; as mentioned earlier, most schools exhibit both strengths and weaknesses. In order to fully satisfy oneself of the suitability of a school it is, therefore, advisable to make a personal assessment.

■ Assessment

Before visiting a riding school, it is worthwhile making a telephone call explaining that you are looking for somewhere to learn. Apart from the matter of common courtesy, this may prove instructive for two reasons:

1. You should, hopefully, be told of a time at which you could expect to watch a lesson relevant to your standard.

2. You can get a very good indication of the school's attitude to new clients.

When it comes to actually visiting the premises, there will certainly be areas on which a novice cannot expect to make judgements, but there will also be much useful information to be gained by simple use of eyes, ears and commonsense. Key points for assessment are:

THE HORSES The mental and physical condition of the horses is of vital importance, and the most fundamental reflection of the standards of any stable. They should appear alert and be of amiable disposition, not showing signs of nervousness, aggression or listlessness. Physically, they should be neither obviously fat, nor thin and 'ribby', and their coats should look clean and healthy. Stabled horses should have a reasonable depth of bedding (usually straw or wood shavings), and the bedding should be fairly clean, dry, and free from unpleasant odour. Inevitably, some boxes will contain the odd pile of recently-passed dung, but there should not be large quantities left unattended to.

Horses being used in lessons should give a general impression of suitability. They should, generally speaking, appear pretty well matched to the size of rider, and be reasonably well-behaved. Although, on novice lessons, some are likely to take mild advantage of their riders (cutting the odd corner, proving slow to

Horses used in lessons should give a general impression of calmness and suitability.

respond to the rider, and generally taking it rather easy) there should be no evidence of animals careering round the arena, bucking, rearing, refusing to budge or attacking other horses. Other points to bear in mind are that the horses should be wearing simple saddles and bridles devoid of gadgetry, and that they should not be excused simple exercises on the grounds of being too young, too old, lame, infirm or incapable.

AMENITIES Riding stables are not hotels, but there is no excuse for their looking like a film set for a First World War drama. There should be lights (in working order) in all boxes and tack room, and a functioning lavatory. The yard, and any walkways, should have good sound footing, and should be well drained (icy puddles in winter being highly dangerous for both horse and rider).

It is a very big plus if the stable has an indoor or covered school, but it should certainly have a well-fenced, properly surfaced teaching arena. It is not acceptable to teach beginners or novice riders in an open field, and, if that is the only teaching area available, then you should give the school a miss.

It is a very big plus if the establishment has an indoor school.

ATMOSPHERE If you are going to spend time and money pursuing any interest, it is important that you do so in an agreeable atmosphere, and the atmosphere of a stable can both influence, and be influenced by, its standards. Surly or miserable staff are a thoroughly bad sign, since their attitude is likely to manifest itself in the standard of their work and, with so many young people being keen to work with horses, such attitudes will usually indicate some major problem with management.

> Good riding establishments usually encourage clients to continue learning beyond the confines of the school itself. Look out for diagrams of horse anatomy, posters advertising lecture/demonstrations and trips to major shows.

On the other hand, too much of a happy-go-lucky or slapdash approach, characterised by vagueness, rides running consistently late, key tasks being performed by children, etc., is unpromising. Apart from the irritation and inconvenience such foibles cause, they may be the precursors of more serious carelessness. Although a regimented, military-style efficiency may be rather overwhelming, a good yard should certainly emit an air of friendly efficiency and you, as the paying customer, should be treated with a modicum of amiable respect, and not as 'just another punter'.

▪ Tuition

So far as the tuition is concerned, a beginner watching a lesson in progress may not be in a very good position to evaluate the technical side of the instruction, but there is still much which can be learnt. Any pupil/teacher relationship is very important, and people of different temperaments and personalities will often prefer different instructors, even though the instructors concerned may be of equal proficiency. The first point to note, therefore, is simply whether you feel that you would get on with the instructor as a person; if you take an instant dislike to them, it is unlikely that you would benefit fully from their tuition, whatever its intrinsic merit.

On a wider basis, it may be worth paying attention to these aspects of the instructor and the instruction.

EXPERIENCE Teaching novice riders properly and safely is a taxing business, which requires considerable concentration, and an ability to foresee and forestall potential problems and dangers. These assets are usually acquired through considerable experience and, therefore, I do not consider that young, newly-qualified instructors *as a group* are especially well-suited to teaching rides of beginners. To continue with this generalisation, it is possible that further difficulties may arise if such instructors are teaching strangers much older than themselves. There is the possibility that they may feel uneasy (and this can manifest itself in over-assertiveness), and they may also be unaware of the difficulties that stiff, unfit people in middle age may face in circumstances which they themselves, or younger pupils, would cope with easily.

While I hasten to emphasise that I am not claiming that no young person can be a good teacher of adult novices, I must also add that any stable which takes the attitude 'it's just a beginners' ride', and leaves the tuition to an inexperienced, unqualified youngster is asking for trouble, and certainly does not deserve the custom.

PATIENCE The instructor who regularly teaches beginners is going to witness a succession of incompetent riders making every mistake in the book, and often rendering it physically impossible for the horse to do their bidding. This is not being disrespectful of beginners – it is merely a statement of fact, as any

Teaching novice riders properly and safely is a taxing business.

honest, experienced rider will remember and admit. Provided, therefore, that the instructor is satisfied that pupils are trying, he must be prepared to exercise great patience, and should not be seen to adopt a theatrical air of resignation, or be rude or dismissive (the 'we know you can't do it so we won't ask you to try' syndrome).

Patience does not, however, include standing passively with a benign smile in the midst of mayhem, or silently allowing riders to persist in flagrant errors or abuse their horses: the instructor must, rather, continue his task in a positive manner whilst 'keeping his cool' in all circumstances.

EFFECTIVENESS This is the essential quality in any teacher, and it embodies many assets additional to those already mentioned. The good teacher must not only have a good knowledge of his subject, but must also have sympathy with the individual requirements and errors of the pupils, and be able to communicate his knowledge in a manner which has maximum impact in each circumstance.

Imagination, humour (if good-natured), tact and an all-round ability to gain the confidence of the pupils are some of the qualities called for, but perhaps the most important attribute of the effective teacher is an ability to explain ideas fully yet concisely. Riding is very much a sport in which it is easy for the teacher to be superficial, to talk in broad concepts without sufficient explanation, or even to take refuge behind a smokescreen of jargon and cliches. The good teacher, however, will take pains to explain *why* actions are right or wrong, and will look to remedy the root causes of errors, rather than their superficial symptoms.

The onlooker should, therefore, hope to see a smooth-running lesson, free from dangerous incidents, in which the impression is that the pupils understand the instructor, and show improvement as a result. Also, the instructor should be seen to divide moments of individual attention as equally as possible amongst pupils, although, if one rider is experiencing particular difficul-

The Instructor should be seen to divide moments of individual attention equally amongst pupils.

ties, the good teacher will tend to spend extra time assisting, while the poor teacher will tend to ignore the problem.

Finally, however efficient an instructor may be, it is a matter of simple arithmetic that, the greater the number of pupils, the less time he can give each individually. Therefore, while riding schools must be expected to put an economic number of pupils on each lesson, the total must remain within the bounds of common sense if clients are to receive value for money and adequately safe supervision. Although hesitant to suggest a hard and fast rule here, I would say that, if rides average six pupils or less, the clients are (numerically at any rate) getting good value, whereas rides which regularly consist of eight or more pupils are becoming distinctly overcrowded.

> A poor instructor will get on a pupil's horse to show off his own skill; a good instructor will do so to demonstrate a point.

COST Although the average cost of lessons is likely to vary as time passes, current 'norms' will always be a useful guide. One should be suspicious of stables which offer tuition at substantially less than the 'going rate', since this may indicate cost-cutting at the expense of the horses' welfare, or manifest itself in worn out or dangerous saddlery, or poor tuition from disgruntled, underpaid staff. Also, it should be borne in mind that riding schools operate as businesses and, while it is necessary for them to be competitive, there is no reason why a stable should undersell itself unless this is the only way in which it can attract custom.

On the other hand, there is no point in paying substantially above the average rate unless the establishments concerned is excellent in all respects, conveniently located, and you can afford it! In my experience, many good schools make no more than an average charge for their services, and the justification of high costs is often related to location rather than excellence of tuition.

Some schools charge by the 'term' rather than by the lesson. Terms, typically, are of twelve weeks' duration, so that there are four a year, with a 'rest week' between each. The idea behind this system is that it provides the school with smoother and surer cash flow, and assists in administration of the stable. Also, since terms have to be booked and paid for in advance, proprietors are protected to some extent from clients cancelling rides at short notice, or just not turning up. With the term system, the arrangement is usually that, if a client cannot attend a lesson, he can 'make it up' on another suitable ride before the end of the term, provided he has given proper notice of cancellation.

The problem with this format, from the rider's point of view, is that is involves a substantial quarterly outlay and commitment, but this may be offset to some degree by the fact that many schools operating the system reduce what would be their hourly rate a little as an inducement. Furthermore, there may be a facility for beginners to have a few 'try out' lessons on a weekly basis before being asked to commit themselves to booking by the term. Although, overall, this system probably favours the proprietors rather than the pupils, I do not feel that a rider should be put off by it, providing he is happy with other aspects of the school concerned.

LOCATION This is obviously an important consideration, but it should not, ideally, be the deciding factor when choosing where to ride. Although ease of access and travelling time and cost have to be taken into account, they should not be considered more important than good, safe instruction and personal enjoyment, and no-one should automatically ride at their nearest school solely on the grounds of convenience.

People living in certain areas will have to recognise the fact that some degree of travel will be essential if they are to ride at all, and, since they will have less choice than normal, it is especially important that they choose their school with care.

▪ Physical Problems and Disabilities

Throughout the rest of this book, the assumption is made that readers do not suffer from any physical condition, disability or illness which would have a serious or lasting effect upon their ability to ride. However, since this may not be true in some cases, I feel that consideration should be given to the position of any reader who, although not entirely able-bodied, is still interested in taking up the sport.

In common with most activities, riding is likely to prove easier for those who are reasonably fit and healthy, but this does not mean that others cannot get a great deal of enjoyment from it, given the right circumstances. The reader may already be aware of the existence of the Riding for the Disabled Association, a charitable organisation with a nationwide network of centres catering for riders with various disabilities. Some of the R.D.A.'s larger centres have facilities for teaching people with a wide variety of conditions, while others specialise in disabilities of which local helpers have the relevant knowledge. It is to the R.D.A.'s great credit that, while they take a very professional and responsible attitude to the safety and welfare of their pupils, there is no air of condescension, and people are encouraged to ride to the highest level practicable – often with amazing results. Although capable of providing tuition for riders with severe disabilities, the R.D.A. does not only cater for the registered disabled; some centres have the capacity to assist those with relatively minor conditions which, nevertheless, might cause difficulty in a standard riding school environment.

Any reader interested in obtaining further information about the R.D.A. can contact them direct at Avenue R, the National Agricultural Centre, Stoneleigh, Kenilworth, Warwickshire.

Choose a stable where there is an atmosphere of care and attention.

With regard to readers who suffer from what might be termed 'general wear and tear', I suggest that they seek out a school which includes a number of more mature riders in its regular clientele and which should, therefore, be attuned to the problems of general stiffness, bad backs, etc. An alternative is one of the commercial schools which sets aside some sessions each week to teach R.D.A. groups and which should, again, be geared up to assist with any peripheral problems. This sort of care in selecting a suitable school is well worthwhile, because there is always a possibility that an establishment unused to clients with physical problems may, through ignorance, take action which results in discomfort or injury to a less-than-fit rider. For the same reason, it is in everyone's interest that any problem or disability is drawn to the attention of both the school and the actual instructor *before* commencing to ride, since it is possible that choice of horse and saddlery may be affected, as well as the actual tuition.

Finally, subject to medical advice and sympathetic instruction, I suggest that anyone who wishes to try riding should do so. Apart from the enormous pleasure the seriously disabled derive from it, there are also many riders around who would probably 'fail the vet', but who nevertheless ride with much enjoyment and success.

■ Personal Risk and Insurance

It is a requirement of the *Riding Establishments Act* that a licence holder must have a current public liability insurance policy, to provide indemnity against damages to persons or property resulting from his, his staff or his client's activities in connection with his business. This is a very sensible requirement but it does not mean that anyone who is injured at a licenced school can automatically expect compensation.

Should negligence or dangerous practice be proven against the school, then that is a different matter, but there is little chance of a claim succeeding in the case of injury or loss occasioned by accident, misadventure or personal negligence on the part of the client. If, for example, a rider has the misfortune to incur injury as a result of simply falling off a well-mannered horse, it is most unlikely that any compensation will be forthcoming.

> If you have the misfortune to be taken ill during a riding lesson, say so and dismount straight away. The back of a horse is a bad place to feel dizzy or faint.

Anyone wishing to insure against such an eventuality should, therefore, consider taking out a personal accident policy, although these often seem to require quite high premiums in consideration of relatively low (and hopefully unclaimed) cover.

— 2 —

THE HORSE

▪ The Need for Understanding

In order to ride well, it is necessary to appreciate fully that the horse is an animal who must be trained to act as a willing conveyance. Much of the sport's fascination is rooted in this fact, but most riders have an imperfect ability to balance their concept of the horse as an animal against their concept of him as a conveyance. Since maintaining this balance correctly in all circumstances is very difficult, failure to do so is not surprising, and is especially understandable in the novice rider, who will tend to be preoccupied with basic problems of technique. However, getting the balance wrong is bound to create difficulties to some degree, and serious conceptual errors will have a markedly adverse effect upon a rider's progress. These errors may, broadly speaking, manifest themselves as follows:

1. Thinking of the horse primarily as a conveyance can result in expectations that he will handle 'mechanically' like a car or a bicycle. This can be a genuine source of frustration and difficulty for someone whose previous experience has been entirely with mechanical vehicles, and also for anyone who believes that there is one strict formula for riding correctly. However, whereas the former are likely to be rapidly dissuad-

A horse is not like a bicycle

ed from their ideas by experience, the latter may persist in theirs and create difficulty for themselves throughout their riding careers.

This state of affairs may come about in a rider who is taught to develop a reasonable posture and basic understanding of how to apply the aids on a well-trained and obliging horse (which is a perfectly good start), but is then unable or unwilling to develop the mental flexibility needed to cope with the demands of riding young, poorly-schooled, excitable or otherwise difficult horses, preferring, instead, to denigrate such animals out of hand. Such a rider will, therefore, not only continue to be restricted in choice of mounts, but will also be unreceptive to the opportunity of furthering his skill and knowledge by riding these horses.

The rider who tends towards this way of thinking should bear in mind that, while there are correct principles of equitation, there is no rigid 'magic formula' technique which will guarantee a correct result from each and every horse, or else prove the horse's worthlessness by its own lack of success. He should, therefore, spend time considering each horse as an individual with regard to physique, temperament, age and state of training, in order that he may develop a better understanding of the animal with whom he is trying to communicate.

2. It is not unusual, especially amongst newcomers to riding, to find those with an over-sentimental view of the horse as a giant pet, to be indulged rather than trained and ridden. People with this attitude doubtless have a genuine affection for horses, but their actions, unfortunately, do not always work in the horse's favour, let alone in their own interests. While an affection for horses is a highly desirable – and almost essential – quality in the rider, it must be tempered with practical considerations if the horse is not to become spoilt.

The beginner or novice with an over-sentimental attitude toward the horse is likely to make slow progress, since he will probably feel that his mount is doing him a favour just by allowing him on his back. Such riders tend to expect little in the way of positive response from the horse, and ride with over-much diffidence, although, strangely enough, this approach does not necessarily exclude the possibility that the horse may still be expected to react 'mechanically' insofar as he is expected to react at all.

In order to obtain improved responses, these riders will need to adapt their approach to the horse somewhat. Although he must not, by any means, be thought of as a slave, it must be borne in mind that active, successful riding involves the horse's willing obedience of the rider, and not vice versa!

We develop relationships with our horses but they are not regarded as pets
to be indulged.

It may, then, assist in resolving these basic imbalances of concept if we consider the horse first in his natural state, and then look at the means and principles by which he may be adapted for riding.

▪ The Horse in his Natural State

The horse developed as a grazing herd animal of the plains. Although various breeds have adapted well to a wide range of environments, their fundamental characteristics have remained pretty much the same: the horse's digestive system is designed to extract nutrients from large quantities of vegetable matter (usually grasses) ingested at regular intervals, and a major function of his physique is to enable him to travel long distances in search of fresh grazing with a minimal expenditure of energy.

A further function of his physique is to enable him to run away if threatened by predators; his other natural defences being security in numbers within the herd, corporate herd reaction to the alarm of one member, well-developed senses of smell and hearing, and the positioning of his eyes.

The horse's eyes, in common with those of many other potential 'prey' animals, are set prominently towards the sides of the head allowing a wide field of vision, the periphery of which is almost behind him. If startled by a sudden movement on the periphery of his vision, the horse's instinct is to shy/run away from it or, alternatively, to kick out with his hind legs. A frightened, cornered horse will often react by turning his rear end toward whatever is threatening him, and some breeds have also developed a skill at defending themselves by striking out with their forelegs.

Although these actions are basically last-line defences the horse will, on occasion, exhibit actual aggression within the herd. The prime example of this is when two stallions fight for herd supremacy, using fore and hind limbs and teeth, sometimes

The horse is a herd animal who finds security in numbers.

to the extent of causing significant injury. The other main example occurs when new additions to the herd are chivvied, nipped and kicked (or hand out the same treatment to existing members) while the hierarchy is being re-shuffled to accommodate them. Mares resisting the unwanted attentions of stallions may also kick out behind, but they (the mares!) would presumably consider this to be defensive action.

These examples of hierarchical unrest may make a herd of horses sound like a potential setting for an American soap opera but, in fact, they represent exceptional behaviour since horses spend most of their time being quite pacific and sociable, some even appearing to develop special relationships and attachments.

All the actions and reactions described above represent examples of a characteristic common to all life forms: that of irritability. In biological terms, this does not refer only to such actions as snapping at flies, but encompasses the very principle of response to all types of stimuli, and it is this characteristic which is of fundamental importance when the question of training the horse arises.

■ Principles of Adapting and Training the Horse

Preparing a horse to be ridden is a vast subject, and many books have been written about specific aspects of training and horsemastership. However, my purpose here is not to go into great detail, but rather to explain *why* the topic should be of interest to all riders. In a nutshell, the explanation is simply that riding is an extension of training and, in order to ride effectively, one must apply and develop the criteria and techniques used in correct training.

Although the beginner or novice may be understandably diffident about thinking in terms of actually training the horse, it must be borne in mind that *all* riding and handling will have some effect upon the horse's education, for better or worse.

It is, therefore, logical and necessary for the rider to look to the principles of training for his own foundation, and, in turn, it is necessary for the trainer to found his own ideas and actions upon a sound knowledge of the horse's psychological and physiological make up. Let us, therefore, look at the fundamental requirements and principles of training, bearing in mind that they will continue to hold good when handling and riding horses.

In order to convert a horse from an unemcumbered herd animal into a willing, attentive and efficient mount, the following criteria must be observed:

1. The horse must lose any fear of human presence, handling or intervention; in fact, the more he comes to welcome them, the better.

2. The horse must, so far as possible, lose any fear of the environment in which he is kept and ridden.

3. He must learn to understand, and be willing and able to accept and perform, any commands or requests of the trainer/rider.

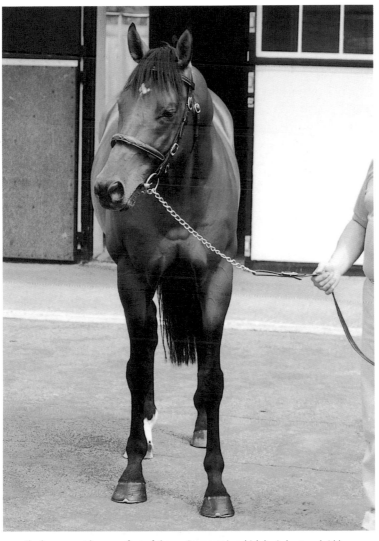

The horse must lose any fear of the environment in which he is kept and ridden.

> Never forget that good riding is ultimately about effective communication with a living creature.

These criteria may involve some subjugation of the horse's natural instincts, and enhancement of his natural physique, and it is essential that tact and patience are exercised by the trainer, who must be sure that he does not ask the horse to do anything which is physically impossible for him, or beyond his comprehension (two factors often ignored by riders!).

While the trainer is in pursuit of these goals, the horse's natural behaviour may work either for or against him in various ways:

FEEDING The horse's need and desire for food can be positively utilised. In the early stages of training, the handler can gain the horse's confidence and trust by feeding him after catching him up, and by giving small edible rewards when the horse responds positively to a specific request. (This is not the same thing as giving tit-bits ad lib, which is counter-productive, and a definite mistake.) At a later stage, schooling sessions can be arranged to finish shortly before feeding time, so that the horse associates work as an activity which is followed by food. At all stages of training, provision of a haynet (the equivalent of allowing the horse to fulfil his natural grazing role) can help keep the horse relaxed in potentially stressful circumstances – being boxed, shod, left alone when other horses have vacated the yard, etc.

In addition to these 'psychological' aspects of feeding, it will also be necessary to change the horse's diet by way of physical adaption. If the horse is to carry a rider as well as moving his own bodyweight around, and especially if he is to do so for long periods and/or at speed, he will require extra strength and energy, and therefore extra nutrition. This will be provided by ensuring that good quality bulk feed (hay and grass) is taken, and by the additional feeding of cultivated cereal crops rich in protein and carbohydrates. However, such a diet must be introduced gradually and with great care, and the amount of 'hard' feed in particular must always remain closely related to the amount of work which the horse is currently performing. This is because, if the extra food is not being utilised to build muscle and provide 'fuel' it can cause serious physical and mental problems in the horse. Nowadays, in fact, it is probable that more horses suffer from the effects of over or incorrect feeding than from being underfed, and correct feeding is something of a science in itself.

HERD INSTINCTS These in particular can be both a help and a hindrance to the trainer/rider. In some circumstances a young horse may be encouraged by working with, or following, older, more experienced horses (on the road, through water, over first jumps, etc.). However, it is necessary to gradually wean the horse away from a dependence upon the presence of others, and to develop his confidence in himself and his rider. Animals in whom the herd instinct remains very strong will always be a source of potential difficulty in situations where they are asked to perform counter to the magnetic attraction of their fellows (standing still while other horses canter past, going 'away from home' at shows, etc.).

The principle of herd hierarchy will continue to function among 'domesticated' horses, and for this reason, care must be taken when riding, or turning a horse out, in unfamiliar company. It is by no means unusual for an animal who is perfectly well-behaved with humans to exhibit aggression towards other horses, and this is a significant source of riding accidents.

DEFENSIVE REACTIONS These are unlikely to be of assistance to the trainer/handler/rider; they are, in fact, more likely to be potential causes of accident or injury, and may interfere with adaptions such as shoeing and clipping, which are normally necessary if the horse is to be worked on various surfaces and in all seasons.

Therefore, it is necessary either to avoid provoking them by incorrect handling or lack of forethought, or else to eradicate them by skilfull training and riding. In some circumstances, where it is essential to overcome an inherent fear of something which must become an everyday object/occurrence, the trainer will gradually and gently insist that the horse makes a closer acquaintance with the source of his fear, rather than deliberately avoiding it. However, if he is wise, he will ensure that the horse already has a good understanding of the aids (signals) by which he may be dissuaded from reacting by attempted flight. It is, for instance, imprudent to start teaching a horse to respond to leg aids when stranded between an angry cement mixer and an oncoming articulated lorry!

Dealing with potentially explosive and spectacular 'flight' reactions (habitual and violent shying, bolting, etc.) is, of course, the province of the experienced rider, and horses who demonstrate such tendencies without extreme provocation have no place in the riding school. However, anyone who handles horses must be aware of the potential dangers of startling, frightening or upsetting even a normally amenable animal; being barged, trampled, kicked or nipped will prove unpleasant even if the horse concerned does so 'accidentally' out of alarm.

There are, therefore, certain principles to be observed. It is always sensible to attract a horse's attention by speaking before approaching and to make the approach, where possible, from an angle between head-on and shoulder-on. Rushing up to a horse or approaching from the rear should be avoided – where it is not possible to move in front of the horse, speaking may cause him to turn round. Friendly tones and a firm, unhurried pat on the neck should help to establish contact, but brash over-heartiness or nervous diffidence will put the horse on his guard.

Sudden movements, loud, unfamiliar noises or any perceived

It takes an experienced rider to deal with explosive 'flight' reactions.

aggression emanating from in front of the horse will normally unsettle him, and he will react, as in his natural environment, either by jumping away or by turning his quarters (rear) toward the source of his anxiety. The same things occurring behind him will cause him to surge forward or to kick out. Handling the rear end of the horse should, therefore, be done with discretion, and, if it is merely required to pass from one side to the other, then this should be done via the horse's front. Where it proves necessary to minister to the nether regions (for example, brushing/bandaging the tail), the handler should work back from the horse's shoulder, using his voice and running a hand along the horse's spine, and he should, wherever possible, position himself at an angle to the hindquarters rather than standing directly behind the horse.

It should be borne in mind that, although relatively thick-skinned, horses not infrequently resent unsympathetic handling of the more sensitive areas, and may react as they would to bothersome insects, by nipping or cow-kicking (kicking forward and outward with a hind foot). Ears, dock and sheath in particular should be handled gently, and brushing the belly area (especially of mares and Thoroughbred types) should be carried out with consideration, and as soft a brush as possible.

In order to avoid the possible consequences of adverse reaction when dealing with the lower regions of the horse, the handler should squat rather than kneel, thus giving himself greater scope for evasive action.

While kindness and patience are key factors in forestalling defensive reactions, this is not to say that there is no place for discipline if the horse exhibits downright disobedience to reasonable and recognisable commands, or if he shows signs of unpleasant and unwarranted behaviour. In such instances, an immediate reprimand in the form of stern, disapproving tones, or perhaps an open-handed smack (or slap with the whip if mounted) may persuade him of the error of his ways. As with children, horses who are used to kind treatment are likely to take much more notice of a rare act of admonishment than those who are constantly bullied or berated and there is, of course, a world of difference between acceptable and justifiable discipline and actions likely to provoke fear, mistrust or violent attempts at self-preservation.

AGGRESSION True aggression towards humans is uncharacteristic of the horse, and real savagery, where it occurs, is often associated with conditions such as brain tumours. Furthermore, apparently aggressive actions are often, in fact, extremes of defensive behaviour engendered by past abuse. Minor (though still undesirable) acts of aggression such as nipping without cause really constitute bad manners, and result from over-indulgence and lack of discipline.

Horses who exhibit genuine aggressive tendencies, for whatever reason, require specialist handling, and have no place in a riding school. However, there are instances where normally safe and useful animals may become 'crotchety' in certain circumstances, and may exhibit aggressive mannerisms without real intent. Their 'warning signs' may take the form of a display of teeth (without actually attempting to bite), stamping of a foot, turning rear end on, and/or the laying back of the ears.

Horses' ears are remarkably expressive, and their carriage is usually an accurate reflection of the animal's attitude. Pricked ears (pointed forward) indicate interest, welcome or happiness, but ears laid back signify unease, dislike or incipient aggression. For this reason, when handling horses, especially in unfamiliar circumstances, it is well worth keeping an eye on their ears.

Horses' ears are remarkably expressive and they are an accurate reflection of the animal's attitude. Pricked ears indicate interest and alertness.

Some horses are natural blusterers, and will look positively murderous in the face of the mildest irritation. Regular handlers will be familiar with such foibles, and able to tell whether or not the horse is bluffing. With unknown animals, however, it makes good sense to exercise extra care and vigilance at all times, although the handler should conceal any feelings of trepidation from the horse.

Understanding, moulding and utilising these behavioural characteristics is an essential and continual part of training, and contributes greatly towards the horse's education for riding. With regard to the actual act of riding, however, it is necessary for the trainer/rider to develop a system of signals which will be recognisable by the horse and, in order to do this, he must understand not only how the horse thinks and behaves, but also how he moves.

— 3 —
HOW THE HORSE MOVES

As with most other animals, the horse's mode of movement is interlinked with both his physique and the demands of his environment. Being a grazing herbivore, he requires a lengthy alimentary canal (digestive tract) in order to extract sufficient nourishment from his diet and, since he may have to travel long distances, or to run for his life, he also needs well-developed heart and lungs. These organs require sizeable abdominal and chest cavities, which have to be enclosed in a reasonably streamlined body in the interests of speed and energy-efficient movement.

While the chief function of the horse's long legs is locomotion, they also serve the purpose of elevating him high enough above the ground to get a good view of his surroundings. This elevation means, however, that he requires a long neck and elongated head in order that he can readily reach down to graze. Being lengthy, quite heavy and 'stuck on the front' of the horse, the head and neck have a significant impact upon his centre of gravity, and thus his balance, and he will often alter the carriage of head and neck as a balancing aid.

The spinal column of the horse, which extends from the head/neck joint to the base of the tail, acts as a kind of flexible

The chief function of the horse's long legs is locomotion. The controlled gallop.

girder, linking the hind and fore limbs and providing a point of suspension for the ribs (and thus the chest cavity). While it could be argued that many parts of the horse's anatomy make an indirect contribution towards movement, the key areas of interest for the trainer/rider are the hind and forelimbs, and the entire length of the spinal column, and it is worthwhile considering their functions and inter-relationships in more detail.

▪ The Limbs

Since it is greatly to the horse's advantage to be tall and fast-moving he has, over the ages, effectively extended the length of his limbs by a modification of the lower legs and feet. His first identifiable ancestor, *Eohippus*, was a five-toed, 'flat-footed' creature but, as succeeding generations found it more expedient to run around on tiptoe, the toes gradually disappeared until, to all intents and purposes, only one elongated toe remained on each foot. The effects of this modification can give rise to confusion if attempting to equate the horse's anatomy with that of a human, especially since there is a tendency to look only at those parts of the horse's leg which are situated beneath the body mass. Although such comparison is perhaps somewhat spurious, it may still be of interest to note, for example, that the joint on the horse's foreleg which is called the knee actually corresponds more readily to the human wrist, and the joint on the hindleg known as the hock (which looks like a 'reverse action' knee) actually corresponds to the human ankle. These relationships will be more readily discerned by studying the locations of the horse's elbow and stifle (patella).

However, regardless of human comparisons or relative terminology, the fact remains that the horse's limbs have developed as a series of powerful, jointed levers, which assist him in covering the ground quickly and with minimal expenditure of energy.

Since he is an animal who moves generally forward in normal circumstances, it is mechanically efficient for the horse to have his main source of locomotive power at the rear, so that he can push/propel, rather than drag himself along. To this end there are groups of large muscles in the hindquarters and upper hind limbs, and the design of the joints in the hind legs enables them to step forward well beneath the body mass.

The shoulders and upper forelimbs are also well-muscled, but their main purposes are to support and balance the horse's forehand (front), and the limbs are designed to move in response to, and support of, the propulsion generated at the rear. If the forelimbs *do* assume the role of major source of locomotion, this is indicative of serious problems, as we shall see in due course.

As well as moving forwards, there will be times when the horse wishes to move in other directions. If, on occasion, he requires to go backwards, he can do so simply by stepping in the opposite direction, but he may also need to turn, swerve or move

Appendicular skeleton (bones of the limbs)

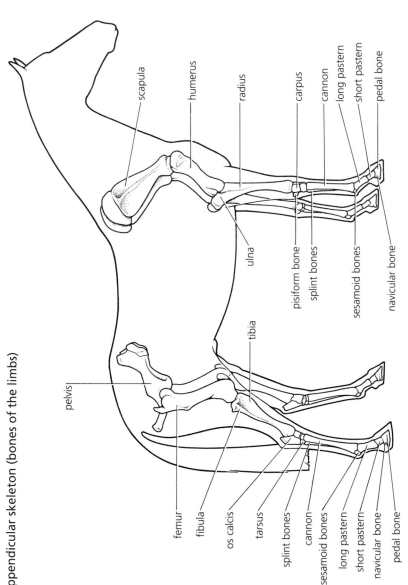

scapula

humerus

radius

carpus

cannon

long pastern

short pastern

pedal bone

ulna

pisiform bone

splint bones

sesamoid bones

navicular bone

pelvis

tibia

femur

fibula

os calcis

tarsus

splint bones

cannon

sesamoid bones

long pastern

short pastern

navicular bone

pedal bone

forward and sideways at the same time. To enable him to perform such manoeuvres the limbs, in addition to hingeing straight back or forwards at the joints, are also permitted by their musculature to move in a manner which allows him, to some extent, to place his feet either 'out' from beneath his body (abduction) or else further underneath than usual (adduction). Such action greatly enhances his manoeuvrability; correctly cultivated by the trainer/rider it can be a considerable asset, but it also provides scope for evading unwelcome commands or situations.

▪ The Spinal Column

This consists of a linked series of vertebrae, and its physical condition and action have a profound effect upon the horse's suppleness and flexibility. The spinal column as a whole can flex in two planes; laterally and vertically.

LATERAL FLEXION The degree to which the spinal column can flex laterally is a key factor in the horse's ability to turn and circle. It used to be considered a principle of equitation that, on a circle, the horse's body (and therefore his spinal column) should be uniformly 'bent' from poll to tail along the circumference of the circle. While this would be mechanically desirable, research has shown that the equine spine is physically incapable of uniform bend along its whole length. In broad terms, tests indicate that, while the front third of the spinal column is capable of considerable lateral flexion, and the 'middle' section of some, the rear section is hardly capable of any measurable lateral flexion at all.

Nevertheless a horse (especially if well-trained and supple) is quite capable of moving on a circle in such a manner that his hind feet step into the prints of his forefeet. The explanation for this apparent inconsistency lies in the horse's ability to abduct and adduct his limbs as previously described, so that he can step either 'underneath' or 'out from' his body. Furthermore, the horse's thorax (ribcage area) is not attached to the forelimbs by any skeletal structure, but is suspended between the shoulder blades by muscular attachments. This allows the thorax a good deal of lateral movement, which contributes to the ability of the horse himself to move laterally.

When a horse moves on a circle what happens, briefly, is that the limbs to the inside of the circle adduct, the thorax itself 'rolls' to the inside, and the limbs to the outside abduct.

Coupled with the actual bend of the horse's flexible neck and the contraction of the intercostal (rib) muscles to the inside, these adjustments create a visual impression of lateral bend throughout the horse.

These processes are however relatively demanding of the horse, because of the effects of centripetal force and the stresses generated within his own body. What he is doing in effect is fighting a tendency for his 'backend' to move off the circle to the outside. If he is not well-trained and ridden, it is likely that he will give in and allow his hindquarters to move outward, destroying the true outline of the circle.

The larger the circle, the less these influences come to bear, and the easier it is for the horse to describe the correct shape. Conversely, because of the mechanical and physical constraints and the sheer size of the horse, there is a limit to the smallest size of circle which he can be expected to perform correctly, and this is usually reckoned to be 6 m (19^1/$_2$ ft) in diameter.

VERTICAL FLEXION The flexibility of the spinal column in the vertical plane has similarities with its lateral flexion in that there is greater flexibility at the front end (neck area), and much less towards the rear. Nevertheless, the spinal column as a whole will tend to form either a series of convex arches (rounded upwards) or else a generally concave (hollow) outline. These outlines have a crucial and interlinked relationship with the way in

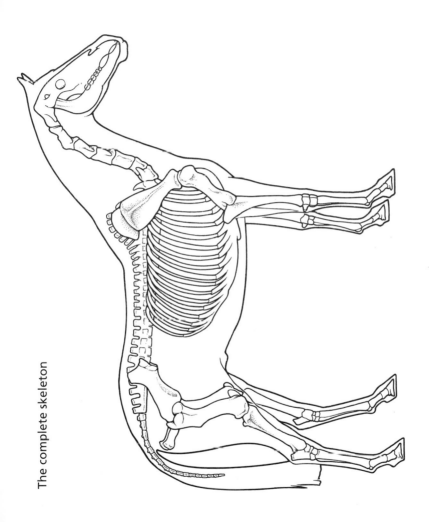

The complete skeleton

which the horse moves his limbs, and it is this relationship which determines his entire capacity for movement.

▪ Relationship between Limbs and Spinal Column

A young, untrained horse of good basic conformation will, when moving naturally, give a general impression of gently rounded outlines of back and neck. Correctly trained, and muscled up into a rider-carrying athlete, these outlines will become more marked. The action of the horse's hind legs, stepping forward powerfully beneath him, will encourage convex elevation of the spine and, since the propulsion will be coming 'from behind', there will be no need for the horse to use his forelimbs to assist by dragging the body along. The action of his forehand will, therefore, be 'light' and free. This 'lightness', coupled with the general convex arching of the spinal column, will tend to produce a graceful curve of the neck, with the head/neck joint beneath the poll relaxed, and the head carried naturally at an angle whereby the face is a few degrees in front of the vertical.

This flexion at the poll, coupled with relaxation of the lower jaw, will be aided and encouraged by correct use of the rider's seat, legs and hands. The overall impression of a horse moving in such a manner will be one of grace, efficiency and power, and the horse's outline, balance and control over his own movements will give the rider the maximum opportunity to control and meter that power by correct and subtle means.

Attempts to produce this state of affairs by short-cuts involving mechanical gadgets (draw reins, etc.) invariably fail because they place too much emphasis upon the front end of the horse (especially head and neck), to the exclusion of the true root of correct movement (hindquarters). Also, such methods are attempting to force what should be a natural process. In unskilled hands, these devices produce an 'overbent' outline of the neck, with an artificially low head carriage and the horse's

Axial skeleton (bones of the skull, spine, ribs and sternum)

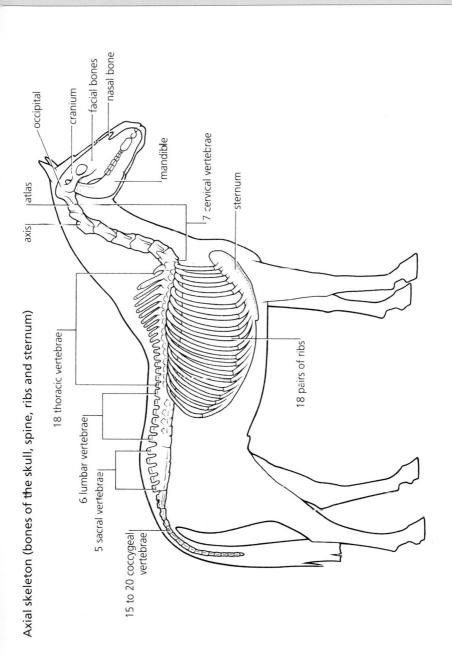

occipital

cranium

facial bones

nasal bone

mandible

atlas

axis

7 cervical vertebrae

sternum

18 thoracic vertebrae

6 lumbar vertebrae

5 sacral vertebrae

15 to 20 coccygeal vertebrae

18 pairs of ribs

face behind the vertical. Since the hindquarters tend to be left to their own devices, and the horse is reluctant to move forward into the leverage being applied to his front end, he will produce as little forward movement as he can get away with; a state of affairs not conducive to success in any equestrian discipline. Unfortunately, this is not the only means by which the horse's movement can be spoilt; any influences which produce a concave outline of the spinal column will seriously inhibit correct locomotion.

If a horse is weak, of poor conformation, or has been badly trained, he may be unable or unwilling to utilise his hindquarters correctly and he will, therefore, rely upon his forelimbs to pull himself along. This condition is known as 'being on the forehand'.

A horse who moves in this way will usually carry his head and neck abnormally low in an effort to balance himself and increase his 'pulling power', and he will tend to 'lean' on the bit and hence feel dull and heavy in the rider's hands. (This feeling is not to be confused with that of a horse who 'pulls' – fights for his head/against the rider's control – through over-excitement.) Despite the low head carriage, the outline of the neck will tend to be somewhat concave, since head and neck will be pushed downward, rather than arched in the manner of a well-trained horse 'having a stretch'. This outline will be reflected in the back, since the hind legs will be trailing and inactive rather than stepping forward under the horse and encouraging upward rounding of the spine.

This condition can often be remedied by a combination of good horsemastership and remedial training, with an emphasis on improving the horse's general condition (and especially that of the hindquarters and limbs) and encouraging him to make greater use of his 'backend'. Even if the horse has naturally heavy shoulders and poor quarters, such methods may still bring about some improvement.

Although the horse who is 'on the forehand' is likely to exhibit some concavity of the spinal column, this outline will be more marked in a horse who is 'hollow-backed'. A 'hollow-backed' horse will, in effect, be 'on the forehand' to the extent that he will make some use of his forelimbs to assist movement, but he will tend to carry his head artificially high rather than abnormally low.

A severely hollow outline may result from physical problems (damaged vertebrae, etc.), but is more frequently caused by bad riding – which may, itself, provoke physical problems.

> Incorrect training and riding are by far the most common causes of bad movement in the horse.

If a horse is habitually ridden by someone who takes a short, fierce hold of the reins, and makes no attempt to encourage engagement of the hind limbs, he will almost certainly adopt a hollow outline, since his main concern will be to avoid the restrictive and unpleasant interference with his mouth. Once in such an outline (the antithesis of the correct, rounded shape), the horse will perform all movements inefficiently and will be very hard to control, both because of the physical constraints upon movement and balance and because his mental state will be one of distress and resistance rather than willing obedience. Unfortunately, those ignorant enough to induce this state of affairs may try to gain control 'artificially' by the use of increasingly severe bits and other gadgetry, creating a cycle whereby it becomes increasingly difficult and uncomfortable for the horse to attempt any forward movement. Horses so ridden frequently and understandably develop such vices as bolting, napping (refusing to go forward) and rearing and, if they do have the good fortune to fall into more educated hands, they will require extensive re-schooling.

The points of the horse

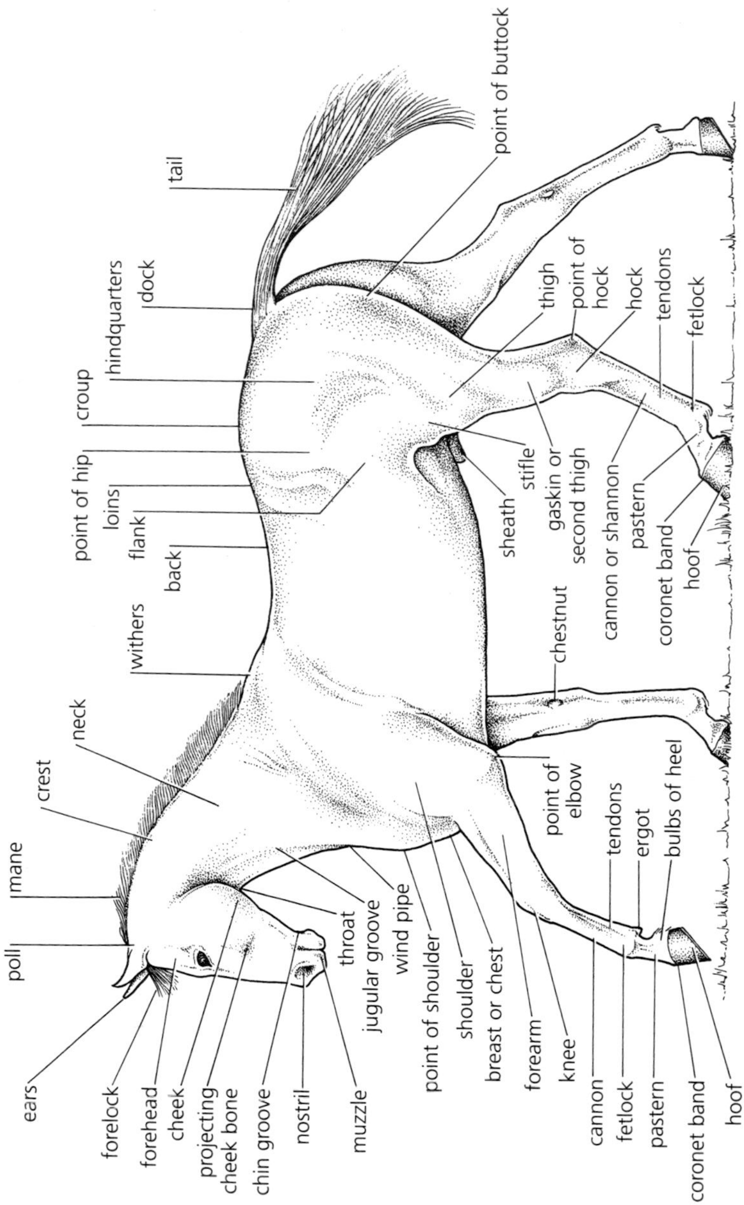

poll

mane

crest

neck

ears

forelock

forehead

cheek

projecting
cheek bone

chin groove

nostril

muzzle

throat

jugular groove

wind pipe

point of shoulder

shoulder

breast or chest

forearm

knee

cannon

fetlock

pastern

coronet band

hoof

tail

dock

hindquarters

croup

point of hip

loins

flank

back

withers

point of buttock

thigh

point of
hock

hock

tendons

fetlock

sheath

stifle

gaskin or
second thigh

cannon or shannon

pastern

coronet band

hoof

chestnut

point of
elbow

tendons

ergot

bulbs of heel

hoof

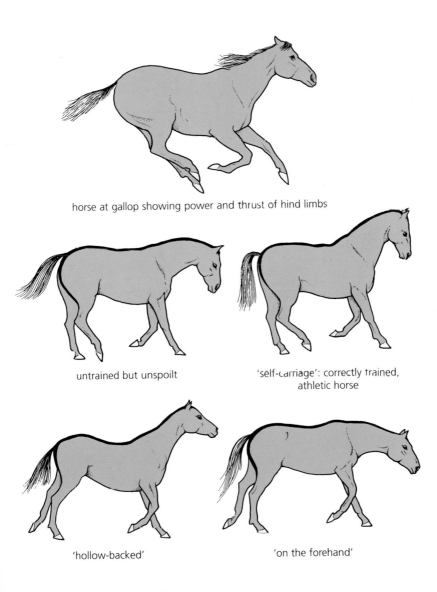

horse at gallop showing power and thrust of hind limbs

untrained but unspoilt

'self-carriage': correctly trained, athletic horse

'hollow-backed'

'on the forehand'

Equine outlines

■ **At the Halt**

The manner in which a horse stands when stationary has a key bearing upon his ability to instigate movement. For this reason, 'halt' in equestrian terminology means something more than 'stand still'; a correct halt is a matter of standing 'to attention'.

If a horse is standing 'foursquare', with both hind feet placed 'underneath' him, rather than left trailing, he is in a posture from which he can readily move into his chosen gait, and in his chosen direction. If, on the other hand, he is standing 'anyhow', it will be harder for him to instigate active movement. Also, if he has one hind leg trailing, this may influence which leg he 'leads' with when he starts to move forward; a factor which may be significant in training and more advanced riding.

■ **The Gaits**

The gaits are the various distinct sequences of footfall which the horse uses for travel. The normal gaits are walk, trot, canter and gallop. Some horses are bred or trained to develop other specialised gaits, but these are very much minority exceptions, and are not dealt with here. The characteristics of the gaits are:

WALK Speed range approx. 5–8 kph (3–5 mph).

Walk is a 'four-time' gait; there are four distinct beats (footfalls) to each stride. These beats should form a regular 1.2.3.4. rhythm, with each foot placed on the ground for the same length of time and with the same amount of pressure. Uneven rhythm, with greater stress on one beat and less on another, may well indicate lameness. A 'marching' (12..34) rhythm is indicative of the horse being bustled out of his correct gait pattern, although horses may adopt a 'slow march' version of this rhythm when walking downhill, especially on slippery surfaces.

The sequence of footfall at walk is one hind leg; the foreleg on

A 'foursquare' halt. This rider is wearing traditional Spanish costume.

The walk.

the same side; the second hind leg; the foreleg on the same side. Because both feet on one side of the horse move in advance of those on the other side, the walk is described as a 'lateral' gait.

Walk may be initiated by movement of a leg on either lateral but, once the gait is established, there is no discernible 'leading leg' or side (i.e. regardless of which hind leg makes the very first step, the established sequence of footfall will always be the same).

TROT Speed range approx. 5–16 kph (3–10 mph), although some breeds/types can trot a good deal faster.

Trot is a 'two-time diagonal' gait. There are two distinct beats to the stride, made by one hind foot and the diagonally opposite fore foot, followed by the other diagonal pair. (To be absolutely precise, in most instances the diagonal pairs of feet do not touch the ground, or leave it, at exactly the same moment, but they are

The trot.

presumed to do so for ordinary practical purposes.) Between the two beats of the stride there is a moment of 'suspension', when no feet are in contact with the ground.

As with walk, once the gait is in motion, there is no theoretical or visually discernible 'leading leg', although many ridden horses will give a feeling of favouring a particular diagonal pair.

CANTER Total speed range approx. 5–24 kph (3–15 mph). Normal speed range approx. 10–24 kph (6–15 mph). Slowest speeds are the province of highly trained horses, and fastest speeds of Thoroughbred types (race horses etc.).

Canter is a 'three-time' gait, there being three beats to the stride in a sequence of: one hind foot; the other hind foot and diagonally opposite forefoot together; the remaining forefoot, with a moment of suspension following the completed stride.

This three-time sequence means that the established gait will have a definite and recognisable 'left' or 'right' aspect. The horse will move either right hind; left hind and right fore together; left fore, or else left hind; right hind and left together; right fore. Having established that it is the hind limbs which provide power and initiate the gait, it may seem rather baffling to discover that the former sequence is described as 'left canter' (or canter on the left leg/rein), and the latter as 'right' canter, references which seem to relate to the last leg (individual foreleg) which completes the stride. However, the reason for this apparent contradiction is that, although the horse is 'rear-engined', he is a fundamentally forward-moving animal, who establishes his direction of travel from the front. This being so, it makes sense to describe as 'left' or 'right' that sequence of footfall which will facilitate moving on a circle/arc in the given direction.

Canter: inside leg leading.

If a horse is cantering on a circle, he will retain balance, rhythm and direction more readily if he is bent in the direction to which he is moving and his primary source of locomotive power (first-moving hind leg) is on the 'outer' rather than 'inner' side of his body. If the primary source of power were on the 'inner' it would tend to push him off the circle to the outside. Also, since his body will be 'bent' laterally to some extent in relationship to the circle, the muscles on his 'inner' will tend to be shortened, and those on his 'outer' stretched, allowing greater freedom of movement for the hind leg on the 'outside'.

A well-trained horse, who is balanced and supple, will, in fact, be able to canter in one direction while on the 'other' leg, but he will not normally be asked to do so other than as an exercise in, or demonstration of, suppleness and obedience (e.g. in a dressage test). This movement, performed intentionally, is known as counter-canter – performed by mistake, it is known as being on the wrong leg! Horses who habitually canter 'on the wrong leg' often do so in one direction only (that is, they will take either left or right canter regardless of direction) because poor training/riding/physical development has rendered it difficult for them to move correctly on one side. Attempts to elicit counter-canter from a horse at too early a stage of training will usually result in his losing balance and falling into a self-preserving trot.

A further refinement of the well-trained horse is an ability to execute a 'flying change' on request. A 'flying change' is performed by the horse utilising the moment of suspension between strides to 'change legs' in the air. This clever and useful manoeuvre is a natural attribute of the horse, and may be used if he makes a rapid change of direction in his free state. Some ridden horses will also perform flying changes as a 'resistance', usually if they are being asked to canter in a more controlled or constricted manner than they are able or willing to comply with.

While it may seem strange that a four-legged animal should

move in a three-time gait, the horse is by no means the only animal to do so, and he is capable of doing so very well. A correctly-trained horse gives a visual impression of great elegance in canter, and this impression will be endorsed by sensations of comfort, ease and rhythm when the animal is ridden.

However, because of the disparity between number of legs and time of gait there is the potential for all sorts of things to go wrong in canter and, given poor physical development, training, riding, or any permutation of these factors, they probably will. Apart from 'wrong leads' and unwarranted 'flying changes', the horse may bastardise the gait in various ways. He may show a trotting action with the hind legs while 'cantering' in front, or vice versa, and he may also 'canter four-time' (splitting the beat of the diagonal pair of legs) or canter 'disunited'. In order to avoid such problems, it is important that the horse's training in canter is not rushed, and that the rider is aware of the concept of 'leading leg', can identify which leg is leading, and can also recognise (feel) the true time of the gait.

The gallop.

GALLOP Speed range: a horse usually gallops when he requires to travel faster than he is capable of doing at canter. An average speed range is approx. 24–40 kph (15–25 mph). Highly-trained horses may be able to show this gait at much slower speeds, and some racehorses can attain speeds of around 64 kph (40 mph) over short distances.

Gallop is a four-time gait, but the sequence of footfall differs from that of walk. In the normal (transverse) gallop, the sequence is one hind foot; the other hind foot; the forefoot on the same side as the first hind; the remaining forefoot. The completed stride is followed by a moment of suspension. The timing of the footfall is such that the hind feet strike the ground in quick succession, there is a pause longer than the time between their footfall, then the fore feet strike the ground in the same succession as the hind feet. The sequence of footfall dictates that, as with canter, there is a discernible 'leading leg' and, for the reasons already described, this is the last foreleg to move. The galloping horse is able to 'change legs' during the period of suspension, although with less facility than at canter. In addition to the association with changing direction, changing legs may also indicate tiredness or unsuitable ground.

REIN BACK It may be stretching a point to describe rein back as a 'gait' within normal equestrian definitions, but if 'gait' may be considered to mean 'method of movement', then rein back is that in which the ridden horse is encouraged to move backwards. In his natural state, the horse may move backwards in various ways (especially if alarmed) but, since the ridden horse must only move backwards in response to a specific command, it is important that he does so in a measured, disciplined manner. The movement itself is somewhat unusual in that it blends aspects of walk and trot. The sequence of footfall is diagonal pairs, as in trot, but the horse steps deliberately rather than springing (there is no discernible moment of suspension), and

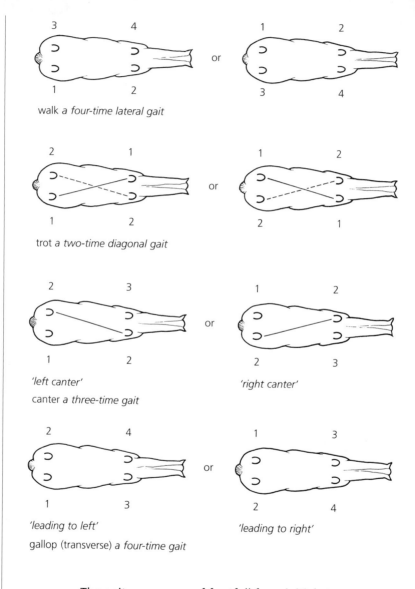

walk *a four-time lateral gait*

trot *a two-time diagonal gait*

'left canter'   'right canter'

canter *a three-time gait*

'leading to left'   'leading to right'

gallop (transverse) *a four-time gait*

The gaits: sequence of footfall from initial step.
At walk and trot, there are not discernible 'left' or 'right'
sequences once gait is established.

the timescale of the stride, and overall speed of approximately 6.5 kph (4 mph) tend toward walk. The general impression is that the horse 'walks backward in trot'.

The horse may move backwards in various ways, especially if alarmed.

The movement is not, however, artificial; it is adopted quite naturally by the horse once he understands the requirement to move backwards and is the method which affords greatest stability, balance and assurance.

▪ Speed and Gait Variations

It will be apparent from a glance at the speed ranges given that there is a distinct correlation between gait and speed – which is why the horse developed different gaits in the first place – but it will also be apparent that there is a considerable overlap of speeds between gaits. Although, for example, a horse's fastest canter will invariably be speedier than his fastest trot, it is entirely possible that he will be able to travel at a moderate speed, for example 10 kph (6 mph) in either gait. This gives rise to two major considerations: why one gait gives a potential for faster movement than another, and how speed may be varied within a particular gait.

With regard to the first consideration, the answer lies in the sequence of footfall (the inherent gaits themselves). The more freedom and potential there is for the hind feet to step fast and far beneath the body, the faster the horse will able to move. To take walk and gallop (both 'four-time' gaits, but at opposite ends of the range) as examples; the 'lateral' nature of walk places obvious limitations upon how fast or far the legs on one side of the body can move in advance of the other side whereas the 'both hind, both fore' sequence of gallop permits maximum use of the propulsive powers of the hind limbs and quarters.

Speed variation within a gait is one of the key issues of equitation. While it would be untrue to claim that all (or most) horses are capable of the full ranges indicated, nevertheless every horse has the potential for substantial variation. This can be brought about either by varying stride frequency (number of like strides per given period) or stride length.

Although the horse certainly can vary stride frequency, this is not desirable in general riding. This is because, within each gait, each individual horse will have an optimum stride frequency at which he is comfortably, pleasantly and efficiently 'active' (a rough analogy would be a motor vehicle having an optimum number of 'revs' at which it can maintain smooth progress in each gear). If the horse's stride frequency is below his optimum he will, in addition to travelling slower in kph/mph, move lethargically; if it is above the optimum, he will travel faster, but at the expense of 'hurrying'. Both circumstances will be detrimental to balance, control, and smooth transitions from one gait to another. The way in which the ridden horse is trained to vary speed within the gaits is, therefore, by altering stride length whilst retaining stride frequency.

There is more to riding than simply obtaining the gait you want: good riding is concerned with the *quality* of the gait – balance, rhythm and speed. Develop the habit, at all gaits, of asking whether the rhythm is constant – and whether it is the rhythm you want.

Although the footfall of the gaits as they go 'up the scale' *allow* for greater maximum stride length, this does not mean that the horse is compelled to take the longest strides possible and, in normal circumstances he will not do so. He will, rather, have a 'normal' active stride length within each gait, and be capable of both shortening and lengthening from this. This shortening or lengthening may, of course, be to any degree within the practical minimum and maximum stride lengths but, with a view to establishing terminology and defining purpose, there are four gait variations recognised in equestrian circles. They are:

COLLECTED Shorter, more elevated steps/strides than normal, with increased action of leg joints. Horse's hind feet usually step a little behind prints of forefeet.

WORKING Normal active stride length, with hind feet stepping pretty much into prints of forefeet. (In walk, this length of stride is associated with a variation known as 'free' walk.)

MEDIUM Strides energetic and above normal length; horse in slightly longer (less rounded) outline. Hind feet step one or two hoof lengths beyond prints of forefeet ('overtrack').

EXTENDED Maximum stride length within correct gait. Hind feet 'overtracking' by three or more hoof lengths.

Since 'working' is the normal gait variation, most readily obtained by horse and rider, it is usual for instructors to base work upon it in the early stages.

Extended trot.

▪ Turning

In normal circumstances, if a horse requires to change direction whilst in motion, he will perform an appropriate part circle (or approximation to it). He is, however, also capable of turning 'in his own length' in the follow ways:

1. By swinging his body around the pivot of the hind leg on the 'inside' of the direction of turn. This movement is known as a (quarter/half/full) turn on the haunches, or (quarter/demi-/full) pirouette. The horse is capable of carrying out such a turn at walk or canter and (if highly schooled) extremely collected trot (piaffe).

2. By swinging his body around the pivot of the foreleg on the 'inside' of the direction of turn. This movement, the 'opposite' of a turn on the haunches, is known, logically, as a turn

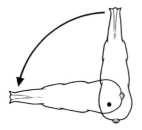

quarter left turn on the haunches

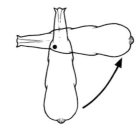

quarter left turn on the forehand

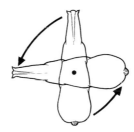

Turns

quarter left turn on the centre

on the forehand. This turn is not observed very frequently in 'free' horses, but is often seen in a tethered horse responding to a handler's request to move round, and is used as a schooling movement to teach horse/rider response to/application of the 'aids'. It is also a most useful manoeuvre for the rider who is obliged to open and shut gates whilst mounted. This turn is ridden/performed immediately following a correct halt.

3. By using his 'centre of motion' (mid-point between fore and hind limbs) as the centre of a circle, and rotating both pairs of limbs round the circumference. This is known as a turn on the centre. The 'free' horse will often perform such a turn in a confined space, and the turn may be ridden from walk, but it is not greatly favoured by instructors because of the temptation for riders to try to pull the horse round incorrectly with the inside rein.

4

FROM STABLE TO SADDLE

▪ Familiarisation

The normal procedure with beginners at many riding schools is for their horses to be tacked up and led into the arena by stable staff, who will assist pupils to mount and then either lead the horses, or walk by their heads, for the first lesson or two. While this procedure is safe and sensible, it can mean that a rider's first real experience of a horse comes only a minute or so before he is expected to mount. This sudden introduction to a surprisingly large, hairy creature can come as something of a shock, and is not likely to assist initial progress.

My feeling is that it would be helpful if more schools gave a little time to introducing pupils to the horse in close up before commencing mounted work (especially since forty minutes or so is quite long enough for a first time in the saddle). Such an introduction could take the form of an experienced member of staff using a friendly horse to demonstrate how to approach an animal in his box, how to ask him to move round, pick up his feet, etc., and how to lead in hand. In addition to providing a practical

Time spent getting to know the horse in his box is never wasted.

grounding in horsemastership, this would promote rider confidence in the horse's presence, and afford pupils an opportunity to experience some degree of control over the horse before having to exercise it while mounted.

Although some schools do this sort of thing, it is probable that the practice is not more widespread because it is felt that pupils have paid to ride, and want to get on with it. This may well be true, but I am nonetheless sure that many novice riders would benefit from a short period of just 'getting used to horses', and I would suggest that any such opportunity be welcomed, rather than dismissed as 'a waste of time'.

While these thoughts are expressed in terms of an initial introduction, it is likely that most schools will, at some stage, offer instruction in leading and tacking up (fitting saddlery). Although these topics are not strictly the province of this book, they are, in practical terms, almost an integral part of learning to ride, and involve aspects of safety and knowledge which are of importance to the rider. I feel, therefore, that it may be beneficial to study them briefly from this viewpoint.

▪ Leading in Hand

Horses who have been well-handled do not usually object to the principle of being led, and the process can be readily demonstrated by any competent person. However, while the safety principles outlined below should be standard practice, I feel that they bear emphasising:

1. If the horse is being led tacked up, the stirrup irons should be run up the leathers and secured. Irons left dangling may not only prove an irritation to the horse, they may also snag on some obstruction in passing, which may both alarm the horse and result in damage to saddlery.

2. Reins/lead rope should be held well clear of horse's and handler's legs. They should not, however, be wrapped/looped round the handler's wrist; this can cause serious injury if the horse does takes fright.

3. The hand near the horse's head (right hand, when leading as normal, from the left) should hold the rein/rope a few centimetres from the bridle/headcollar. The fingers should not be looped through the bit rings or headcollar. Again, this can result in injury in adverse circumstances.

4. When turning the horse, he should be turned away from the handler (to the right when leading from the left) in as large an arc as circumstances permit. Not only is this easier for the horse – it avoids the possibility of his treading on the handler's feet.

Leading a pony correctly.

5. At all times when leading, remain at the horse's shoulder: do not walk on ahead of him, paying out the rein behind you. Not only may this cause the reins to loop dangerously, it also surrenders control of the situation and prevents you from being aware of the horse's actions and reactions.

6. Novice handlers should not be expected to lead young, excitable or otherwise difficult horses, nor should they be required to lead on public roads. However, even normally well-behaved horses may react adversely to frightening objects, the unwarranted attentions of other horses, or even the overwhelming attractions of the feed room! The handler should, therefore, remain alert at all times, looking ahead for potential problems, and giving them as wide a berth as possible. Asking the horse to walk on actively, using encouraging tones of voice and turning his head somewhat away from the source of difficulty can all prove helpful in such circumstances.

▪ Tack and Tacking-up

It is important that pupils receive proper and thorough instruction in this field, and are not merely regarded as a source of free labour. It is one thing for a riding school to provide correct tuition in tacking up, and to allow clients to tack up well-mannered horses once competence has been established (and subject to checking). It is an entirely different matter to give a 'one-off' crash course, and then expect clients to operate unsupervised, possibly with different horses and equipment. This latter approach can and does lead to accident and injury, and is indicative of a slipshod and careless attitude wherever it occurs.

The actual process of fitting tack is more readily learnt from practical example than from the written word, an experienced person being able to demonstrate simple procedures which may sound quite complicated in abstract. It is not, therefore my pur-

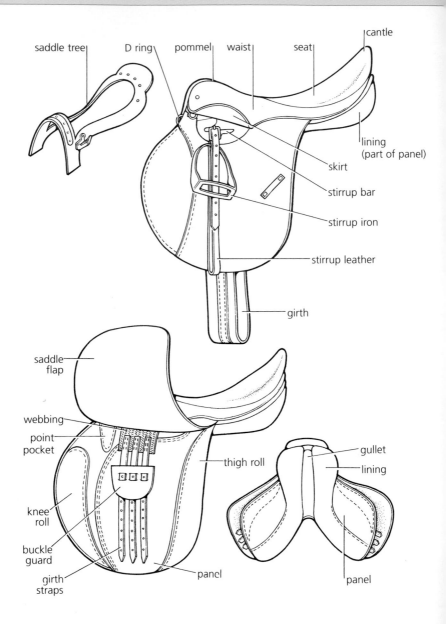

saddle tree | D ring | pommel | waist | seat | cantle

skirt

stirrup bar

stirrup iron

lining (part of panel)

stirrup leather

girth

saddle flap

webbing

point pocket

thigh roll

gullet

lining

knee roll

buckle guard

girth straps

panel

panel

The parts of the saddle

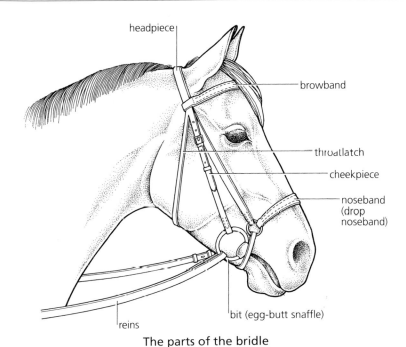

headpiece

browband

throatlatch

cheekpiece

noseband
(drop
noseband)

bit (egg-butt snaffle)

reins

The parts of the bridle

pose to study the mechanics of tacking up, but rather to outline some general, but important, principles. These are:

CONDITION OF TACK While one cannot expect riding school tack to be brand new or permanently gleaming, it certainly should be safe, serviceable and reasonably clean. However, rather than taking this for granted, it is in the rider's interests to get into the habit of checking tack from an early stage. Although, at first, the knowledge to assess fitting and adjustment may be lacking, there are some important basic points which do not require equestrian experience: all buckles and stud fastenings should be in good condition, and properly fastened; all stitching should be in good condition; nothing should be twisted and nothing should be excessively worn, torn or cracked (in addition to leather items, bits and stirrups irons can wear and crack, and 'irons' – especially cheap nickel ones – can become twisted or bent).

If circumstances permit, it is a good idea to check that those parts of the saddle and girth which come into contact with the

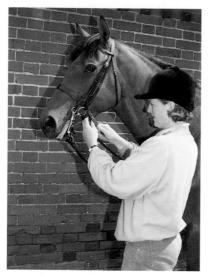

horse are clean and undamaged. This is important not only in terms of the horse's welfare, but also because of the possible effects his discomfort may have upon his performance.

Obviously, once the rider does acquire an understanding of correct fitting and adjustment of tack this will help his cause, and any opportunity to further one's knowledge in this field should be capitalised upon.

Instruction should cover the correct fitting of tack.

SUITABILITY In addition to being in good condition, tack supplied for a novice rider should be both suitable of itself, and indicate suitability of the horse to whom it is fitted. Normally, it should consist simply of snaffle bridle, general purpose saddle and neckstrap. Should the conformation of the horse warrant it, then provision of a breast girth (to stop the saddle from slipping back) or crupper (to stop the saddle from slipping forwards) is obviously sensible. Some schools fit running martingales in an attempt to regulate the rein aids regardless of the position of the rider's hands. While I doubt that this practice enhances the rider's education, it has to be said that it may sometimes make the horse's task more tolerable.

However, items of tack additional to, or at variance with the above tend to make matters look dubious at least. Although it may be a harsh judgement, the wearing of protective boots and bandages in the school tend to suggest that the horse may not be sound enough, or move well enough, to be a safe conveyance for a novice rider. Provision of a bit other than a snaffle is definitely inappropriate, and the practice of fitting a pelham on a young, unbalanced or over-keen horse with the intention of converting him into a 'novice ride' is indefensible, and invariably detrimental to both horse and rider. Hackamores (bitless bridles which operate by pressure on the nose) are also unsuitable for novice use, especially in cases where they are fitted short-term to a horse with mouth trouble (and therefore not regularly ridden or schooled in such a device).

Of course, it is also important that the 'normal' tack suits the rider. Reins must not be so short that they cannot be 'slipped' (allowed to run through the fingers if the horse is to be given a 'long rein') without fear of losing them, nor so long that the spare section loops dangerously near the rider's foot. Very fine reins, common in riding schools (presumably on grounds of cheapness), are *too* thin for most adults to hold without tightening their grip and thus 'deadening' hands and forearms, and they can become dangerously useless when wet and slippery. Dry, stiff and dirty reins, especially the plaited type, can cause a surprising degree of soreness and blistering of the hands.

This horse is wearing a 'D' ring snaffle bridle.

The correct and comfortable fit of a saddle is crucially important so far as the horse is concerned, but the saddle will also have a marked influence upon the rider's comfort, posture and effectiveness. There are various styles of saddle, of which the 'general purpose' is most suitable for novice riders. Jumping saddles (which are designed with a forward cut panel and substantial knee rolls) are fine for their purpose, but tend to make it difficult for the rider to retain an appropriate leg position when riding with a normal length of stirrup on the flat. Conversely dressage saddles, while designed specifically for flatwork and useful for the experienced rider, tend to be built on the assumption that the user has already developed a deep-seated 'long-legged' posture, and they may create strain and insecurity in the rider who has not yet reached such a stage.

Style apart there are, unfortunately, some very bad saddles made, in which it is very difficult to be comfortable or retain a good posture. Many schools, in fact, have a notorious 'rogue' saddle (often so acknowledged by the staff) which seems to survive either because it happens to fit a particular horse passably well or because of the cost of replacement – neither reason being of much comfort to the client whose lesson is ruined.

While one should be very wary of blaming the saddle for any or all postural deficiencies, there can be times when it is very much the culprit. Should you feel this to be the case, and find that the instructor declines to acknowledge that it is so, it may be worth suggesting that he tries riding in it himself.

In addition to the saddle itself, the stirrup leathers and irons must be appropriate. The leathers must be of such length that they are capable of adjustment to suit the rider's requirements, and the irons must not be so small that there is a risk of the feet becoming wedged in them, nor so large that the feet could readily slip right through.

The neckstrap is simply a leather strap (such as a spare stirrup leather) fitted loosely round the base of the horse's neck; its purpose being to provide something for the rider to hold on to should he lose his balance or feel insecure. It is *not* the purpose or function of the reins to provide such support, as we shall see in due course. In normal circumstances, it should be unnecessary

The saddle should fit both pony and rider and stirrup irons and leathers should be appropriate. This is a show pony wearing a saddle with a straight flap designed to show off the animal's shoulders.

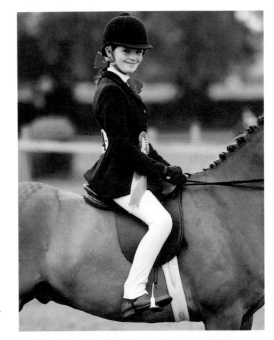

BELOW This horse is out hunting and the saddle flap is cut forward with a knee roll to assist the rider over fences – the reins are covered with pimpled rubber to prevent slippage.

This pony has a stirrup leather round his neck for the rider to hold if necessary.

to actually use the neckstrap but, if it is needed, then it may prove invaluable. Additionally, its mere presence can give a beginner a greater sense of security, and thus lessen the possibility of destructive tension and stiffness.

It seems surprising that more schools do not habitually provide neckstraps for novice riders, a common alternative being to tell a pupil in difficulty to hold on to the front arch of the saddle.

While this can be an effective measure, it is not likely to be an instinctive one, and, too often, the rider is already in trouble before this course of action is mentioned. While I do not wish to dwell on potential problems at this stage, I feel that it would be helpful if, at the start of the first mounted lesson riders were told that if in difficulty, they should not haul on the reins (or fling themselves around the horse's neck!), but sit up straight and hold the neckstrap firmly in one hand. This could prevent a lot of bruising to horses' mouths and riders' bodies.

FINAL CHECKS There are two safety checks which the rider should always make before mounting:

1. That the 'safety catches' on the stirrup bars are *down*. The stirrup bars are the steel arms by which the stirrup leathers are attached to the saddle. They normally have spring catches at the end, and these should always be left down (in the horizontal position) so that, should the rider fall off with a foot caught in the stirrup, the leather will pull away from the saddle and prevent him from being dragged.

The stirrup bar should remain straight to enable the stirrup leather to slip off in an emergency.

2. That the girth is sufficiently tight to prevent the saddle from slipping when mounting. This check should be made immediately before mounting, after a few minutes riding, and occasionally thereafter. (Some horses are past masters at 'blowing themselves out', and the girth may need adjusting two or three times.)

Checking their tack never did anybody harm – not checking it might well do!

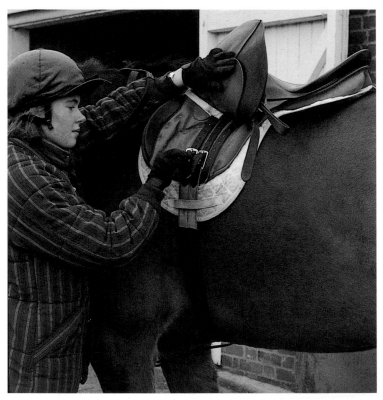

Check that the girth is sufficiently tight to prevent the saddle slipping when you are mounting.

▪ **Mounting**

Mounting should be a simple process, provided the rider is reasonably able-bodied and the horse is not unduly large for him. However, while every rider should, in due course, learn to mount unaided (and from either side), it is always helpful to have assistance and, in the early stages, this is essential. It is also sensible to make use of a mounting block whenever one is available, since this makes the business that much easier and more comfortable – especially for the horse.

There are several slightly different ways of mounting, but they all involve putting the left foot in the stirrup (when mounting from the nearside) and springing up, swinging the right leg over the horse's quarters. In order to do this with a minimum of fuss and effort, the following points should be borne in mind:

1. Ensure that the left stirrup is adjusted so that you can place your left foot in it without undue strain. If the horse is on the large side for you, this may mean taking the leather down a few holes more than your estimated riding length. Do not, however, be tempted to take it down too far, or you will have trouble swinging the right leg high enough to clear the horse's back, and may also 'lose' the left stirrup immediately after mounting.

2. Horses do not greatly enjoy having a rider's toes dug into their sides during the mounting process. Therefore, if the required stirrup length and the horse's conformation suggest that there is a chance of this happening, it may help to start off facing more towards the horse's front than usual, and angling the left foot in the same direction.

3. Before actually mounting, ensure that the horse is standing still. This is where an assistant can be most helpful but, when one is not available, it will be necessary for the rider to use the reins in the left hand to maintain a halt. This involves

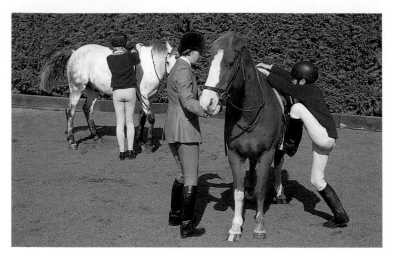

An assistant holds the pony whilst the rider practises mounting.

keeping a definite, but not over-harsh contact with the horse's mouth. If the horse shows a tendency to move away from the rider, it may help to shorten the right rein a little.

4. The act of elevating oneself into the saddle is greatly facilitated by standing close to the horse with the right leg 'underneath' the body, and *springing* from the right leg – after one or two preliminary hops, if necessary. Most riders who experience difficulties when mounting do so because they do not use the right leg sufficiently; they try to climb into the saddle by putting excessive pressure on the left stirrup and/or hauling on the saddle with the right hand. Not only are these methods inefficient, they are uncomfortable and unbalancing for the horse, and cause extra wear to the saddlery. The rider who does need to assist himself with the right hand – beyond merely resting it on the saddle – should hold the front arch and not the cantle (back of the saddle), since this can cause the tree (central skeleton) to become twisted or broken, which will necessitate a very expensive repair.

— 5 —

BASIC TECHNIQUES AND PRINCIPLES

▪ Criteria for Good Riding

Now that we have dealt with the basic psychology, physiology and movement of the horse, we are in a position to look at equitation from the rider's point of view. Before going on to discuss the techniques and principles of riding, however, it is worthwhile establishing a clear picture of what the rider is trying to do, and forming some perspective of the learning process.

Good riding is dependent upon the following criteria:

1. The rider must sit in harmony with the horse, so that his mount is best able to carry himself and the rider in comfort and balance and with the minimum of physical effort.

2. The rider must communicate his desires to the horse in a manner which the horse will readily understand and accept; and he must not apply aids which contradict each other.

3. The process of communication must be two-way; the rider must be sensitive to the signals he receives from the horse. In addition to realising when he has the horse's obedience/co-operation, the rider must learn to interpret signs of confusion, difficulty and incipient disobedience, in order that he may take the appropriate action.

4. Although, at times, the rider may ask the horse to do something which he will find mentally or physically taxing, the
rider must not make impossible or unreasonable demands of
his mount.

*Learn to interpret signs of confusion and
difficulty in the horse.*

Together, the theory and practice of these criteria highlight
the paradox that riding is both a very simple and very complex
business. The simple theory which may be distilled from them is
that riding is a matter of sitting correctly on the horse, giving
him signals that he can understand (which must necessarily be
simple) and obey, and evaluating his responses. There is nothing
wrong with the logic of this theory and it will, in fact, be valuable if it can be borne in mind at all times, since it may promote
clarity of thought in moments of difficulty.

However, it seems that it is often difficult to do something
simple well, and riding is a prime example of this. The complex
nature of the sport becomes apparent when we attempt to put

the simple theory into practice, and set about actually trying to sit correctly and communicate effectively. We shall look into these matters more deeply in due course but, for the moment, the complexities can be summarised thus:

1. A complete beginner may, under competent instruction, achieve what looks to be a very reasonable riding posture at halt during the first lesson. However, a major requirement of sitting correctly – a 'deep' seat – involves muscular adaptations in the rider's thighs, posterior and pelvic area and, at a more advanced level, a knowledge of how to use and control these muscles. To achieve such adaptation and understanding necessarily takes a considerable time. Furthermore, the 'deep' seat and good posture are not only important in themselves; until they are obtained, the rider will not be in a position to apply the aids to optimum effect.

2. Although the aids are limited in number, and simple in concept, they can be applied with many different nuances and in many different combinations, and may elicit many shades of response from the horse. They are, in effect, the 'language' by which the rider communicates with the horse. While any language is based upon the simple building blocks of an alphabet, it takes time to learn sufficient vocabulary and grammar to communicate to any degree, and a lifetime may be spent in improving and refining communications: this process is mirrored in the relationship between rider and horse.

It is, therefore, physically and mentally impossible to 'learn to ride' overnight, or even within a set period. Indeed, if one were to ask top horsemen from any sphere 'are you still learning to ride?' it is likely that they would all have the honesty to answer in the affirmative.

Because of these factors, individual variables, and the tempta-

It can take a long time to master the language of communication between rider and horse.

tion to assess progress in terms of 'riding hours' rather than results, I am reluctant to offer any arbitrary timescale of progress. However, since I appreciate that newcomers to riding may find a broad outline of the early stages useful, I shall cite the experiences of my own riding club members in connection with the British Horse Society's Grade Tests. These tests are amateur examinations in riding and horsemastership, which may be taken by members of clubs affiliated to the B.H.S. There are four progressive tests (I–IV), the first two of which might be loosely designated 'novice'. The 'general requirements' stipulated for these are: Grade I – 'rider must be capable of riding in an enclosed space, on a quiet horse, and of assisting in getting a horse ready to be ridden'; Grade II – 'rider must be capable of riding a well-mannered horse alone or in company, and of assisting in the stables'.

Members who have joined the club as beginners, and have received a regular hourly lesson each week, with perhaps a few extra sessions have, almost without exception, passed the Grade I test if they have taken it after a year or so. Of those who have attempted Grade II after two years upward, the majority have been successful. I would stress that this information is not given with the intention of suggesting either above or below average standards, but because it has the merit of being established fact and may, therefore, be a more useful guide than any timescale based on conjecture or assumption.

It is probably reasonable to say that many riding clubs would recognise Grade II standard as being on the verge of 'average club rider' status but, reverting to my reluctance to suggest timescales of achievement, I must add a very strong warning at this point. This level of ability is *not* indicative of 'having arrived'; rather, it indicates that the rider has reached a basic level upon which he can build through further learning and experience, and begin to work toward participation in the various equestrian sports (dressage, show-jumping, cross-country, etc.) which may capture his imagination. I would therefore ask the reader, in his own interest, to bear in mind the need for continual progress as we proceed to examine the basic techniques of riding.

▪ First Thoughts in the Saddle

In the interests of safe and effective riding it is a good general principle for the rider to show himself to be in control from the moment of mounting. He should, therefore, make any adjustments necessary to stirrups, etc. without delay, and start working the horse gently forthwith. He should not get into the habit of fiddling about for several minutes and/or allowing the horse to meander aimlessly on a long rein; this will cause the horse to think that he is carrying a passenger rather than a rider and, sooner or later, the rider may encounter a horse on whom such a lackadaisical approach is positively dangerous.

However, while this principle should be borne in mind by all riders, the beginner will be concerned with more fundamental thoughts, and will also have assistance in keeping the horse at halt while the basic elements of posture and control are explained. Since the first few minutes on a horse are obviously of great importance for a newcomer to riding, it is worth examining some common attitudes and reactions, and discussing their potential influences on the rider's progress:

MISLEADING PRE-CONCEPTIONS When a human being is confronted with a new situation, he will inevitably seek to evaluate it in the light of any existing information at his disposal. While this characteristic can be of immense value, it can also create problems if the information to hand is incorrect or misleading. So far as riding is concerned, it is highly likely that this will be the case. For instance, virtually everybody who has never sat on a horse 'knows' that 'you kick it to make it go, pull both

A common fallacy is that 'you kick a horse to make it go, and pull the reins to stop'.

reins to stop and pull one rein to turn'. To the viewers of most Western movies, this will seem to be irrefutable fact, but it is the sort of idea which must be thoroughly exorcised from the mind before any progress will be made in equitation. Equally, the rider should shed any vague memories of a distant day's pony trekking, and blot out lurid reminiscences of casual-rider friends ('I went riding a couple of times, but the horse kept stopping to eat/bolted/threw me/was on loan from a taxidermist').

▪ Instinctive Reactions to New Sensations

When seated on a horse for the first time, the rider will have a definite sensation of being 'high up'. In fact, his head will only be a further half a metre plus from the ground than if he were standing erect, but the sudden change from normal experience may make the difference seem greater than this. Another sensation will be the sudden awareness that he is sitting astride a living creature who, even at halt, can act of his own volition. The horse's actions will, no doubt, be quite normal and harmless; he may, for instance, stretch his neck to rub an itching nose against a foreleg, or look round and inspect the rider's boot. Their significance lies not so much in the actions themselves but rather in the rider's realisation that he is about to attempt control of a conveyance capable of independent thought.

These sensations, possibly coupled in the rider's mind to a vague idea that he might fall off or make an exhibition of himself, may well produce some feeling of 'insecurity' in the first moments. In using the term insecurity, I am not implying that the rider is likely to experience fear, but rather referring to a perfectly natural (although hopefully unwarranted) mental reaction to novel circumstances over which the individual feels that he has, as yet, little control. The problem is that the physical responses which may be triggered by such feelings are likely to prove counter-productive both in terms of real security and riding technique. These responses are:

GENERAL STIFFNESS AND TENSION Stiffness and tension in the rider tend to block/harden the lines of communication with the horse, reduce the chance of physical harmony (unless they cause mirror-effect stiffness and tension in the horse, which is obviously undesirable), and cause the rider to bounce around in the saddle when in motion.

TAKING A DEAD, FIERCE HOLD OF THE REINS We have already touched upon the fact that the reins are not provided for the rider to hang on by, and any attempt to do so will cause the horse considerable discomfort, make his task of standing or moving correctly difficult or impossible, and possibly provoke resistances which will not assist the rider's security. Furthermore, consideration of the horse apart, an assessment of the mechanics of the situation will show that attempts to achieve security via the reins is impractical. If the rider requires to hang/pull on something to secure himself, then logic dictates that he must choose an object which will pull him closer to the horse (neck-strap or saddle arch). The only direction in which he can pull on the reins is up and backwards (i.e. *away* from the horse), and the only direction in which the reins could pull him is forward and down (i.e. over the horse's head).

GRIPPING STRONGLY WITH THE LEGS, AND DRAWING THEM UP This is the most logically understandable reaction of the insecure rider. After all, the legs are long powerful limbs, and

The reins are a means of communication with the horse. They are not there for the rider to hang on by.

seem ideally suited and situated for the purpose of clinging to the horse. Furthermore, the rider may already have heard of the principle of keeping the legs 'on' the horse at all times, and think that a general feeling of insecurity justifies substantial extra pressure. It is true that, as the rider progresses, he may experience moments when a considerable degree of grip is necessary; for instance if the horse shies, plays up or stumbles badly. However, to be fully effective in such circumstances, the grip will need to be centred in the rider's upper legs and combined with an 'adhesive' seat, and the problem with leg grip as applied by inexperienced riders is that it tends to be centred on the lower legs. The drawbacks of this are:

1. The application of substantial leg pressure represents a crude signal to the horse to move forward quickly and suddenly, and will come at a moment when this reaction is almost certainly contrary to the rider's wishes.

2. Attempts to grip strongly with the lower legs tend to be accompanied by the legs being drawn upward. This is probably an instinctive reaction intended to create grip on the widest part of the horse, and to achieve greater grip with the knees, but it actually lessens the security of the seat and general posture. Mechanical analysis will show that a significant contribution to the rider's security is made by the fact that he has a long, heavy limb hanging symmetrically each side of the horse, placing a good deal of weight below his own centre of gravity. Drawing the legs up will detract from this mechanical stability, tend to loosen the rider's seat in the saddle, and may also result in him losing his stirrups. It can even create a snowball effect where the rider feels insecure, draws his legs up, becomes more insecure, draws his legs up further, and eventually works himself right off the horse.

If, then, the rider is aware of the adverse effects of these attitudes and reactions, he will be better primed to subjugate them, and to concentrate upon attaining a correct posture, and the security which it affords.

▪ Posture

The key benefits of correct posture are:

1. It promotes rider security.

2. It permits the rider's weight to remain stable on the appropriate part of the horse's back, thereby assisting the horse and enabling the rider to remain in harmony with him.

3. It places the rider in a position from which he can apply the aids to maximum effect.

These elements are crucial to effective riding and it is, therefore, most important that the correct posture is a 'natural' one, that is,

· Good seat posture and leg position.

it can be maintained without strain or discomfort. This does not, of course, mean that *any* posture adopted 'naturally' upon mounting will necessarily be correct. In fact, riding problems may be caused/aggravated by instructors allowing pupils to assume their own postures in the saddle, and then attempting to correct them 'in parts' while the pupils are riding. Logic suggests that it would be easier for all parties if more emphasis were placed upon correct posture from the outset, especially since it can be practised and 'felt' firstly without recourse to a horse, and then established 'in situ' at halt.

In order to practise the riding posture dismounted, all that is required is to stand upright, straight-backed but not artificially stiff, with the feet together ('to attention'). Both feet should then be moved equidistant sideways so that they are about shoulder-width apart, with the toes still pointing forwards. The head should then be inclined just enough to glance downwards, and both knees flexed until they virtually obscure the toes from vision. The head should then be returned to an upright position, looking straight ahead. The resulting posture, comfortable, balanced and readily-maintained is, in all major respects, the correct riding posture. It should remain substantially the same when performing various school movements at walk, trot and canter, although it will be adapted to cope with the varied demands of jumping, and when riding in the open at fast canter and gallop.

Since body posture must be the sum of inter-related parts, each having an effect upon the other, it is important to understand *why* a particular posture is correct, that is, how it makes

There is a general tendency for novice riders to pay too little attention to the importance of sitting correctly. A rider who is unbalanced, whose involuntary movements unbalance the horse, and who prevents the horse from moving correctly by 'hanging on' has no chance of sending the correct signals.

the parts of the body mechanically efficient in producing the key benefits mentioned above. Let us, therefore, examine the main body areas in these terms:

THE SEAT In equestrian terminology 'seat' means rather more than just 'backside'; it encompasses all those parts of the rider's anatomy which will normally be in direct contact with the saddle, together with all directly related and connected bones, muscles, etc. In broad terms, the main constituent parts are the thighs, buttocks and pelvis, but the lower part of the spinal column (up to and including the lumbar vertebrae) may also be included in the definition, since this area provides the crucial link between 'seat' and 'back' which affects not only posture but also the application of 'seat and back' aids.

The seat, being the rider's main physical link with the horse, is the keystone of the whole posture, and it is therefore essential that it is correctly established. Although a well-made saddle has a correct area (the lowest part) for sitting in, and its design will

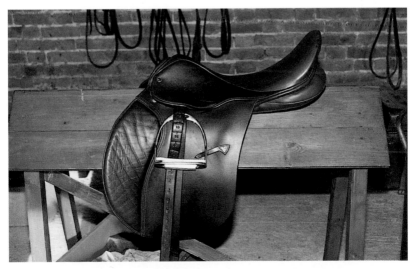

A well-made saddle is designed to encourage the rider to sit in the deepest part.

encourage the rider to do so, it is by no means impossible for the rider to sit incorrectly, especially if his stirrups are wrongly adjusted, and he is attempting to take his postural 'point of reference' from his feet. This is why it is so useful for the rider to have

The thighs should be flat against the saddle.

thoroughly established a 'feel' of the correct posture before mounting, in order that major departures from this can be recognised and remedied. The key points of a correct seat are: that the thighs (thigh muscles) are 'flat' against the saddle, holding firmly, but not with a fierce, taut grip (except in emergency); that the rider's backside is positioned in the lowest part of the seat of the saddle; that the rider has a definite feeling of sitting on his seatbones (the base of each side of the pelvis), with equal weight distribution on each, and with as large an area of the seatbones as possible pressing down towards/into the saddle. This may not, in all honesty, feel very comfortable at first, but the rider should avoid trying to 'ease' the seatbones by tipping or rocking forward or backward, since this will destabilise the seat and hence the whole posture.

(There are times in riding when it may be appropriate to ease the weight and balance of the seat somewhat toward the front of the seatbones, for instance when riding a young horse, jumping, or riding at speed in the open. However, such an action should be part of a conscious and purposeful adaptation of posture for a specific reason – other than to relieve a sore backside!)

THE UPPER BODY In all normal circumstances the upper body should remain still and erect (although not stiffened), thus assisting the rider to remain in balance and harmony with the horse. The rider will be able to use the resultant straight back to optimum effect when applying 'seat and back' aids. In order to assist (and not adversely affect) the straight back posture, the head should also be held erect, looking ahead rather than down.

As an aid to maintaining correct upper body posture, instructors often tell pupils to 'elevate the rib cage' (sometimes embodied in the instruction 'grow taller above the waist'). This is sound advice provided that the rider understands that this is *precisely* what he is being asked to do, and does not seek to 'grow taller' by lightening his seat and/or 'standing up' in the stirrups.

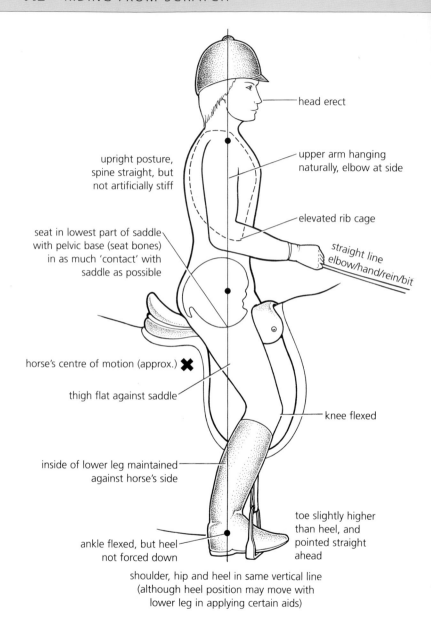

head erect

upper arm hanging naturally, elbow at side

elevated rib cage

upright posture, spine straight, but not artificially stiff

straight line elbow/hand/rein/bit

seat in lowest part of saddle with pelvic base (seat bones) in as much 'contact' with saddle as possible

horse's centre of motion (approx.) ✖

thigh flat against saddle

knee flexed

inside of lower leg maintained against horse's side

toe slightly higher than heel, and pointed straight ahead

ankle flexed, but heel not forced down

shoulder, hip and heel in same vertical line (although heel position may move with lower leg in applying certain aids)

Basic elements of good posture

THE LEGS It is important that the length of the rider's legs dictates the length of stirrups and not vice versa, otherwise incorrect leg position may occur, affecting both the application of leg aids and the rider's overall posture.

There is an old 'rule of thumb' for assessing the practical length of stirrup for any individual, which suggests that the length from stirrup bar to base of stirrup iron should equal the length of the rider's straight arm, from knuckles of fist to armpit. This seems to work out quite well in most cases, and will provide the novice rider with a guideline accurate to within a hole or so. When put into practice, however, it is worth remembering to adjust the offside stirrup as well as the nearside, since it may be necessary to alter the nearside leather from one's 'riding length' to facilitate mounting.

The other 'rule of thumb' for assessing stirrup length is the knee just about obscuring the toe from vision, mentioned earlier. With experience, riders will readily recognise the 'feel' of appropriate stirrup length, although they may still wish to adjust them (hopefully downward) during the course of a lesson. However, while it is desirable for the rider to get 'longer in the leg', this should result from a genuine 'deepening' of the seat, and the novice rider should not attempt, or be persuaded, to ride with overlong stirrups, since muscle strain and insecurity may result. It is normally preferable for stirrups to be *slightly* too short, rather than too long.

The purpose of the stirrups is to assist the rider's balance and security but, in normal circumstances on the flat, they should do so very much as an adjunct to the seat, and their role will largely be one of 'safety back-up'. However, in the early stages, their mere presence is likely to assist and encourage the rider and, correctly adjusted, they may also play some part in helping to retain a good leg position.

The more advanced rider will, however, be able to ride quite happily on the flat without stirrups, and riding for short periods

It is better for the stirrups to be slightly too short (left) than too long (right).

in this fashion is an exercise commonly used to help riders who are past the initial stages to further 'deepen' their seats. It is interesting to note that riding without stirrups usually causes less difficulty than riding with over-long stirrups for which the rider is continually 'reaching'.

If, then, the rider's seat and stirrup adjustment are correct, the legs, continuing down from the thighs, should naturally hang flat against the horse's sides. This means that the *insides* of thighs, knees, calves and ankles should rest against the horse, with the toes pointing straight forwards. The feet should be placed in the stirrup irons in such a manner that the balls of the feet (just behind the base of the toes) rest on the irons. The flexion of the knee and ankle joints should be natural and supple, not forced and stiff, and the flexion of the ankles will result in the heels being slightly lower than the toes. The stirrup leathers should hang down vertically, and the lower leg should rest 'on the girth', with the ankle joint vertically beneath both hip joint and shoulder (although the lower leg may move from this juxtaposition during the application of leg aids).

THE HANDS In equestrian terminology the word 'hands' is often assumed to include the arms as well. The hands provide, via the reins, an important and delicate link with the horse's 'front end'. While this link requires that the hands be 'quiet', it does not require that they remain fixed rigidly in one position, and when considering the hands under the general heading of 'posture' it is important to avoid any such inferences.

The purpose of discussing the hands at this juncture is to establish the method of holding the reins, and to look at the general positioning of the hands and arms which results from this and from the upper body posture. The normal method of holding single reins is for the rein to run from the bit, between the little and third finger of each hand, then across the base/bottom joint of the fingers, emerging between finger and thumb, with the thumb resting on top of the rein. The loop of spare rein should hang out of the way down the side of the horse's wither (preferably the side to which the whip is not being carried). The basic reason for the single rein not running round the little finger is to leave this finger free to divide the double reins of a double bridle. However, my feeling is that the 'three finger' hold of a single rein also promotes greater sensitivity. Regarding sensitivity, the basic hold of the reins should be light but firm as if, for example, holding a valuable glass object which must be neither dropped nor crushed.

In order to provide a continuous and useful link with the horse, the length of rein must remain such that there is a light but definite feeling of 'contact'; that is to say that the rider must retain the ability to 'feel' the bit in the horse's mouth, and the horse must be able to 'feel' the rider's hands. Therefore, while the reins should in no way be 'pulled tight', there should be no discernible slack in them while the horse is being actively ridden.

The consequent straight line from bit to hand should normally be continued along the forearms to the elbows. These should rest close to the rider's sides, as a result of the upper arms hanging down naturally from still shoulders. The precise angle of the bit – elbow line will depend upon the horse's head carriage which, in turn, will be influenced by a number of factors (conformation, state of training, rider's intentions, etc.). These factors may result in the rider's forearms being carried at any angle from almost horizontal to the ground to up to about 45 degrees below horizontal. It is not, therefore, possible to talk of a hard-and-fast 'hand position' but, as a general guide, the 'average' position of the hands will be about 5 to 8 cm (2 to 3 in) above the wither.

To continue the principle of direct link between hands and horse's mouth, it is usually appropriate for the hands to be carried about the same distance apart as the width of the mouth: 12 – 13 cm (about 5 in). However, if the horse has an unusually thick neck/mane, it may be necessary to extend this distance just sufficiently to avoid any undesired interference with the rein contact.

The hands should normally be held on the same level, with the thumbs uppermost; the knuckles should not be turned skywards since this will prevent the correct articulation of the wrists when giving aids, and will also tend to twist and tighten the muscles of the forearms. Although, during the application of aids, the wrists will flex at angles to the forearms, they should not be habitually fixed at an angle; the 'norm' (from which they may flex as and when required) is the natural positioning with the back of the hand appearing pretty much as an extension of the forearm. The overall feeling of hands and arms should be light, supple and natural; there should be no heaviness, stiffness or forcing of positions.

▪ Errors of Posture

These frequently do not manifest themselves until horse and rider are in motion, and this may, therefore, seem an early juncture at which to examine them. However, the reasons for so doing are:

1. Since they obviously contradict the principles of correct posture, it seems sensible to examine errors while the correct principles are still fresh in the mind.

2. Postural errors do not *necessarily* occur only in motion, and if they exist at halt, they are inevitably going to get worse once horse and rider start to move.

Errors of Posture do not manifest themselves until horse and rider are in motion.

3. If the rider has a prior awareness of postural errors and their consequences, he may take greater care to avoid allowing them to develop.

4. Once the rider is in action (probably in company with several others), the instructor – being only human – may find that time and mental resources are at a premium, and he may, therefore, tend to slip into the habit of pointing out peripheral symptoms of incorrect posture without analysing the root cause and fully explaining its impact. This approach may persuade the pupil that the error is less significant than it actually is, with the consequence that he either continues to exhibit the error until serious problems result, or else absorbs it into his technique to the general detriment of his riding.

> Errors of posture are not errors of style, but errors of effect.

A major aspect of postural error is that, since the parts of the body are closely connected, an error in one area is virtually certain to adversely influence other areas, creating, to some degree, an overall 'bad posture'. These 'bad postures' can be ultimately categorised into body tipping forwards, body tipping backwards or body tipping sideways, each with attendant problems and consequences.

However, these categories are rather broad and the rider may not, at first, consider them to be particularly significant – thinking of them rather in the same light as the peripheral symptoms mentioned above. It may, therefore, be useful to analyse the common errors of posture from their various sources, in order to establish their inter-relationship and assess their impact.

ERRORS ORIGINATING IN THE SEAT
1. *Sitting on back of saddle and rear of seatbones.*

Seat tending to give permanent crude 'driving' aid, encouraging hollow outline of horse's back. Upper body tilted back behind vertical, out of harmony with horse (behind his 'centre of motion' – midway point between hind and fore limbs). Hands artificially high and far back (in response to upper body posture) either 'hanging on' to reins, aggravating 'hollowness', or else abandoning rein contact altogether. Legs either tilting or thrust forward to counter-balance upper body, and therefore in a position which seriously restricts the application of leg aids. This overall posture has similarities to that which may be adopted instinctively in an emergency (for instance, if the horse stumbles badly) – the crucial point being that, in such circumstances, the rider *must not* retain a short hold on the reins. However, as a posture for general riding, it is ugly and ineffective.

2. *Tilted forwards onto crutch.*

This position in the saddle weakens the security of the seat and inevitably causes the upper body to tilt forward, reducing or negating the use of seat and back aids, and allowing the rider to be easily pulled forward by a keen horse. If the rider's spine curves, rather than just tilts forward, these adverse effects become much more marked. The ability of the seat to absorb the effects of the horse's motion is lessened or lost, so that the rider will tend to bounce around in the saddle, destroying harmonious movement and further weakening his position.

Hands may either be planted on the withers (to prop the rider up), adversely affecting rein contact, or else the rider may seek to use the reins for support, holding them artificially high and clutching them to his chest. This will either destroy the forward movement of the horse (if he is lazy, and seeking an excuse to stop), or else cause him to react by pulling back against the rider; a contest which, with the rider in this posture, the horse is certain to win.

The forward pivoting of seat and upper body will result in the legs swinging back and up, and being used to grip rather than to apply aids. This type of posture, even in its milder forms, will considerably reduce the rider's ability to control

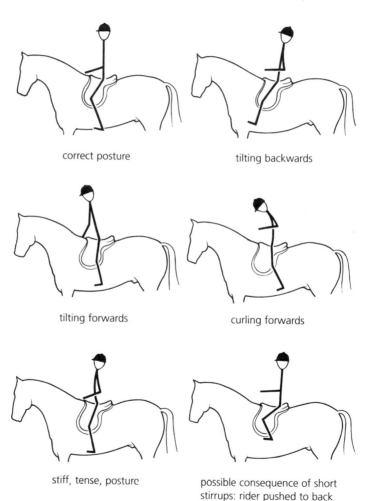

correct posture

tilting backwards

tilting forwards

curling forwards

stiff, tense, posture

possible consequence of short stirrups: rider pushed to back of saddle

Postural errors

his mount and, in its more extreme forms, it will render any significant degree of control impossible, and prove highly precarious – to the extent that the rider will be likely to fall off at the slightest provocation.

Equitation aside, there are obvious physical drawbacks to this posture, especially for male riders.

3. *'Tight' seat, with tensed thighs/clenched buttocks.*
Attributable to the general stiffness mentioned earlier. Renders seat incapable of absorbing the effects of the horse's movement, and results in the upper body jolting/bouncing around in the saddle; movements which are reflected involuntarily in the hands.

4. *Sitting crooked.*
Seat tilted to one side or the other, with unintentionally different pressure on seatbones. Tilting often reflected in hips, shoulders and, perhaps, hands. Rider out of balance with, and unbalancing, horse, who will seek to regulate his load by stepping 'underneath' the 'heavier' side of the rider (consequently, one cause of 'crookedness' in the horse).

ERRORS ORIGINATING IN THE UPPER BODY

1. *Leaning back behind the vertical.*
Creates the effect of sitting on the rear of the saddle/seatbones, with the same results.

2. *Leaning or curling forwards.*
Even if the rider merely looks habitually downward, rather than ahead, the weight of the head will induce this posture to some extent. It will cause the rider to at least tip onto the front of the seatbones and, to some degree, create the problems of the 'crutch seat'.

3. *Over-stiff upper body.*
This may be directly related to the 'tight' seat, but may also

result from an exaggerated attempt to sit erect – like a small boy playing soldiers. Even if the root cause of the stiffness does not include the seat as such, stiffness in the upper spine will be reflected in its lower regions (lumbar vertebrae), resulting in jolting of the upper body and stiff, unsteady hands.

4. *'Dropping' a shoulder or 'collapsing' a hip.*
Often related to a tendency to 'lean in' round corners, or to 'desperate' application of a leg aid. Is inevitably reflected in crookedness of seat, with results as described.

ERRORS ORIGINATING IN THE LEGS

1. *Errors related to incorrect stirrup length.*
Having the stirrup leathers at other than optimum length will not inevitably cause postural error, but it increases the likelihood, especially in the novice rider whose seat and posture are not 'established'.

Riding with stirrups too short (in the context of flatwork) may tend to push the rider to the back of the saddle, if he puts too much weight in the stirrups and allows the lower leg to swing forward. Riding with stirrups too long can result in the rider rocking from side to side as he perpetually 'reaches' for the irons. Alternatively, in an attempt to secure them, he may either straighten the legs forward, 'locking' himself on the back of the saddle, or else 'stand' in the irons and weaken his seat.

Pre-occupation with retaining the stirrups generally results in ineffective leg aids.

2. *Thrusting the legs forward.*
Creates the effect of sitting on the rear of the saddle/seatbones. As we have seen, this may form part of an emergency act of self-preservation, but it is counter-productive in terms of normal riding.

Thrusting the legs forward creates the effect of sitting on the rear of the saddle.

3. *Drawing the legs artificially far back.*

From the point of view of applying leg aids, there are times when it might be to the rider's advantage to be able to draw the legs back further than most people can manage. In this respect, the rider who is sufficiently supple to apply such aids *without weakening his seat* probably has some advantage.

Many novice riders take some time to establish their correct length of stirrup leather. There are good reasons for this – early feelings of insecurity, tight leg muscles, undeveloped seat muscles, adapting to the shapes of different horses. It is therefore normal that some time is spent trying to adjust the leathers. Learning to do this one-handed, with the feet in the stirrups will minimise time spent 'fiddling about'.

However, some instructors seem to have become obsessed with the possible advantages of such a leg position, and encourage pupils to ride with their legs habitually further back than their physique really permits. Not only does this throw undue strain upon the leg muscles, hip-joints and lower back, it also frequently results in the rider tipping forwards into the 'crutch seat' already described. It should be borne in mind that the leg position will gradually move 'back and down' as a natural consequence of the seat 'deepening' through riding experience. While this is most desirable, arbitrary attempts to force the issue are to be avoided.

4. *Legs turned outwards.*

This posture is most immediately noticeable by the position of the toes, which turn out because the rider is using the back

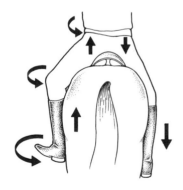

Postural consequence of turning toes out; right leg shows correct position and influences; left leg shows movement of foot reflected throughout whole leg.

Legs too far back result in the rider tipping forwards into the crotch seat.

of the heels (instead of the inside of lower legs) to give aids – or even as a source of grip. The consequence of turning the toes out is that the whole of the leg, from ankle to hip, also turns out to a degree, thus weakening the thigh area of the seat. An extreme consequence is that, with the seat weakened and the heel being virtually the only part of the leg in contact with the horse, an impasse is created whereby the insecure rider grips harder with the heels, thus undermining his position further.

THE HANDS Although it is true that actions such as riding with the reins too short or carrying the hands abnormally low may result in the upper body tilting forward, 'errors of posture' in the hands do not generally have the same impact upon the overall position as do errors in the other parts of the body. Provided that the shoulders remain still, the actions of the hands may be either appropriate or inappropriate to the application of rein aids, but they will not directly affect the rider's position.

However, it is apparent that the hands may be very sensitive *indicators* of postural error in other areas; a connection which is often overlooked. Although the hands and arms are naturally very mobile, the shoulders act as a fixed point which must, inevitably, move in accordance with any movement of the upper body. If this upper body movement were voluntary, it might be possible for the hands to remain still (the movement being absorbed by changing angles in the joints of the arms). However, it is very difficult, or impossible, to fully absorb *involuntary* movements in this manner – as anyone who has attempted to write during a train journey will confirm!

Since upper body movement related to postural error – i.e. bouncing/rocking around in the saddle – is involuntary, it is inevitable that it will be reflected in the hands; unsteady hands being, therefore, almost invariably symptomatic of bad posture. For this reason, isolated exhortations to 'keep your hands still' are usually pointless; what is required is for the underlying postural error to be identified and corrected.

▪ Posture When the Horse is in Motion

In order that the correct posture can be maintained when the horse is in motion, it is necessary for the rider to be able to use his seat as a 'shock absorber' to prevent the natural movements of the horse from causing instability. The essence of a shock absorber is that it allows movement into itself and then absorbs it, and the rider must think of his seat in the same light. Any attempt to use the seat as a rigid 'defence' against the horse's movements, or to avoid them by moving the seat away from the saddle, will result in various of the postural errors previously described.

The agents of 'absorption' in the seat are the buttocks, the muscles of the pelvic region and, to some degree, the thighs. These are assisted in their task by correct posture, especially of the spine and lower back.

The ability to employ these agencies correctly and usefully is gained gradually, as the rider's practical awareness of the horse's motions increases, and his physique adapts to the demands of riding. One of the consequences of sound instruction and riding experience will be that the thigh and buttock muscles will adapt more readily to the shape of the saddle, and the seat will physically 'deepen', so that the rider might be said to be sitting 'in', rather than 'on' the saddle. This condition, where the seat 'wants' to stay in constant contact with the saddle, is described in various terms ('glued/stitched to the saddle', 'adhesive seat'), and represents the foundation stone upon which good riding may be built. Progress towards attaining such a seat will be assisted by attention to correct overall posture, and by performing

OPPOSITE The walk is the easiest gait at which to retain the posture established at halt.

various exercises which will form part of a good instructor's curriculum. Lunge lessons (discussed later) can be a particularly useful medium for these aspects of learning.

The precise manner in which the seat will act to absorb the horse's movements will vary from gait to gait (and also from horse to horse and with the gait variants). Let us, therefore, look at the general effects of the gaits upon the rider, and consider how they can be dealt with.

WALK Walk is the easiest gait at which to retain the posture established at halt. The 'lateral' sequence of footfall will manifest itself through the horse's back as a series of gentle forward movements of alternate sides, each followed by a slight lateral roll. These movements will be readily absorbed if the seat is kept

supple, but, if it is either too tense or too sloppy, the rider's upper body will reflect them (the 'closing time' syndrome).

As a natural consequence of the gait, the horse's head will move slightly forwards and backwards, and, in order to retain a constant rein contact, the rider's hands and forearms must remain 'soft' and supple, and respond to this movement. It is most important that the response is in direct relationship to the movement; arbitrary 'rowing' motions of the hands are to be avoided.

TROT From the rider's point of view there are two ways of performing trot; 'sitting' or 'rising'.

Sitting trot is normally employed when riding 'school' movements, and at any other time when the rider wishes to remain in the optimum position for exercising control and applying all the aids as required. The rider should always sit to the trot for at least a couple of strides after a transition into the gait, or before a transition into a different one. In sitting trot, the rider's seat remains in the saddle, absorbing the motion of the gait, and the rider should appear to be simply sitting still in the posture already described. At trot, the horse's head should remain steady, and the rider's hands should do likewise. (If a horse 'nods' at trot, this is a sign of lameness.)

Since, in trot, there are only two 'beats' to each stride, it is inherently the least smooth of the gaits, and the 'feel' through the horse's back is in marked contrast to the gentle motions of walk. It may, in fact, feel distinctly bumpy at first acquaintance, and the novice rider is likely to require some practice before he learns to absorb this movement in his seat, and can perform a correct sitting trot. This is best achieved by ensuring that the posture is correct in walk, and then asking for a few strides of trot, with one hand holding the front arch of the saddle to assist in maintaining contact with the seat. The rider should try to 'allow' the movement into his seat, and should therefore make a

Learning to ride at trot will defeat posture to start with.

conscious effort not to clench the buttocks or draw the legs up. Although it may take a while to achieve success, the effort will be rewarded not only in respect of being able to sit to the trot correctly, but also in terms of the progress made towards obtaining an 'adhesive' seat, will the all-round advantages this confers.

If performed for long periods, especially on hard or uneven terrain, the motions of trot can be quite physically demanding of both horse and rider. The principle of 'rising' to the trot was originally developed to alleviate these demands in an age when the horse was a major means of transport, and long rides under such conditions were commonplace. Nowadays, 'rising' trot is still used primarily in similar circumstances (trotting on roads or across country), and is also frequently employed in the early stages of training young horses in the gait. To execute (correct) rising trot, the rider deliberately eases the weight from the rear of his buttocks/seatbones on alternate steps of the two-time gait, that is to say he 'sits' on one diagonal and 'rises' on the other. This movement should be of the rear of the seat only, and should be made, both in terms of timing and degree, in direct response to the movement of the horse (i.e. in harmony). As a consequence of the easing of the seat, the upper body may incline forwards *very* slightly. While the thighs may assist in taking the weight momentarily eased from the seat, there should be no influence of, or from, the lower legs, and the rider should certainly not seek to remove the whole of his seat from the saddle by 'standing' in the stirrups. It should, in fact, be perfectly possible to perform rising trot without stirrups and, while a novice would not be expected to get this right 'first go', the more experienced rider who finds this difficult has instant proof that he is performing the movement incorrectly.

Horses, like humans, tend to be either 'left' or 'right' handed. Consequently, when trotting, most will favour one diagonal or the other, and the rider will feel more comfortable if he 'sits' on the favoured diagonal. However, in order to prevent the horse from becoming 'one-sided', the rider should spend an equal amount of time on each – and more time on the 'uncomfortable' diagonal if he wishes to take remedial action. He should, therefore, 'change the diagonal' at frequent intervals and this is achieved simply by 'sitting' for one extra beat/step. If rising trot is performed in the arena (where the horse will be frequently circling or turning), it is usual to assist his balance by 'sitting' on the diagonal in which the outside hind leg is stepping 'underneath' the horse, and the inside foreleg is stepping forwards. With a little practice, the diagonals can be readily 'felt', but, in the early stages, the visual check is to 'sit' as the *outside* shoulder moves back (if the outside foreleg is moving back, the inside foreleg, and its 'diagonal' hind leg, must be moving forward).

Although the extent to which the rider eases his seat in rising trot should be the minimum commensurate with the horse's movement, the action of 'rising' inevitably results in trading some degree of control for mutual comfort. However, if the rising is performed incorrectly, the result will be that the rider sacrifices both control and balance to his and the horse's discomfort.

Errors in rising trot almost invariably result from the rider rising too high (usually with 'assistance' from the lower legs), thereby forfeiting all contact with the seat and getting out of rhythm and balance with the horse. This may result in his tipping either backwards or forwards, with the attendant postural disadvantages. One problem peculiar to exaggerated rising trot is that continual use of the lower legs for 'rising' will render them ineffective for applying aids, and efforts to urge the horse forward when 'rising' in this fashion will just result in the rider rising even higher.

It seems likely that a major cause of these errors is the tendency to teach rising trot before sitting trot. The reasoning behind this practice appears to be that the novice rider will find sitting trot difficult and uncomfortable, and he should therefore be taught rising trot as a means of avoiding the motion. However, although the main purpose of rising to the trot is to make trotting less demanding in certain circumstances, this dodging of the issue does not seem very constructive, and, because the rider has not yet developed any real 'feel' for the motion, and is thinking in terms of escaping it, he is likely to 'rise' incorrectly, creating more problems than he solves. Furthermore, if a rider thinks along such lines, his negative attitude to the movement will make the adjustment to 'sitting' that much harder, both physically and mentally, whereas the rider who has learnt to 'sit' correctly should have little trouble in adapting to rising.

In order to ride to any reasonable standard, the pupil is going to have to learn sitting trot at some stage, and, for the reasons

Don't brag about 'getting the hang of rising trot' – do so when you have got the hang of sitting trot.

examined, this should be as early as possible. However, in view of the probability that the reader will, in fact, be taught rising trot first, it is hoped that an awareness of the potential pitfalls will help in avoiding them.

CANTER (flatwork in the school). Often described as the most comfortable and pleasant gait to ride and, performed correctly on a well-trained horse, this is quite true. However, the fact remains that riders often find canter (especially on a less well-trained animal) a difficult gait to sit into, and they end up performing a sort of bumping 'rising' canter, which is generally uncomfortable and unbalancing for both horse and rider.

The source of the difficulty lies in the natural motions of the gait which cause the horse's back to move down, forwards, and up in sequence (even when the horse is moving in a correct, 'rounded' outline). Unless the rider has developed a reasonably deep and 'adhesive' seat, this movement is likely to result in the

The canter is often described as the most comfortable gait to ride.

saddle 'escaping' downwards, the net effect being that the rider will appear to move up, back and down, out of rhythm with the horse.

The rider should, then, *allow* his seat to move with the saddle, but he should not think in terms of generating his own arbitrary movements. The unseemly thrusting motions of the pelvis habitually made by some riders are most unlikely to be in real accord with the horse's movement, and the consequent rocking back and forth of the upper body will only result in loss of harmony and unsteady rein contact.

This type of movement may also be employed in a misconceived attempt to use the seat as a 'driving' aid, and is often observed in those on horses who are reluctant (for whatever reason) to move forwards into the rein contact. While the seat can have a role to play in encouraging forward movement, this role must be a subtle one, employed in conjunction with the legs; loss of harmony and unsteady hands will not cause a poor canter to improve!

Attention should, therefore, be paid to keeping the upper body still and erect, and using the legs as the primary influence for maintaining forward movement.

GALLOP Riding at gallop can be enormously exhilarating, but it should not be done carelessly, or by a rider of insufficient experience. Gallop is the gait the horse will naturally adopt in moments of extreme excitement or fear, and he must be correctly trained and ridden in the gait if he is not to make associations with such instinctive reactions. Therefore, although the primary objective of galloping is to go fast, this does not mean that the rider should abandon control; on the contrary, it is crucially important that control is properly maintained.

This dual emphasis on speed and control is the key to the rider's posture at gallop. We have established that major functions of posture are to assist the horse by remaining in harmony and balance, and to place the rider in a position of security and control, and these principles hold good at all gaits. However, the nature and demands of gallop are such that is necessary for the posture to be adapted from the 'norm' in order that these criteria may be met. Before looking at *how* the rider makes the required adaptations, it is important to understand why they are necessary.

The key to this lies in the two 'centres' which influence equine movement; the centre of motion and the centre of gravity. We have already touched upon the centre of motion, the mid-point along the horse's spine between the hind and fore-limbs. This is located roughly beneath the base of the rider's own spine when he is sitting erect in the saddle; an important and useful juxtaposition for applying 'seat and back' aids.

The centre of gravity is a fluid point. With the horse standing correctly at halt, it will be located vertically beneath his spine, at a point close to the (normally seated) rider's knee. This location results from the horse's conformation in general, and his long head and neck in particular. However, it is influenced by gravity itself, and by changes in physical outline and the effects of acceleration/deceleration. Therefore, once the horse starts to move, the centre of gravity will move also. Its precise location will change almost continuously with the stride cycle and any changes in speed but, at gallop, these factors will tend to move its 'average' location forward to a degree.

When the rider requires the horse to travel at speeds near to his maximum, it follows that, once the gait is established, he should make the horse's task as easy as possible by placing the burden of his own weight as close to the horse's centre of gravity as is practical (although *never* in front of it). Given the approximate centre of gravity, it is apparent that this will involve the rider moving his upper body forwards and down. However, we have already seen that tilting the upper body forward can result in various postural errors, the most serious being curving the spine, and a tendency for the lower body to tilt backwards. The first of these errors can be avoided by the rider ensuring that he *folds* forward from the hips, keeping the back straight; the second, however, cannot be readily resolved from the starting point of a 'normal' posture.

The reason for this is that, in the 'normal' posture, the rider's

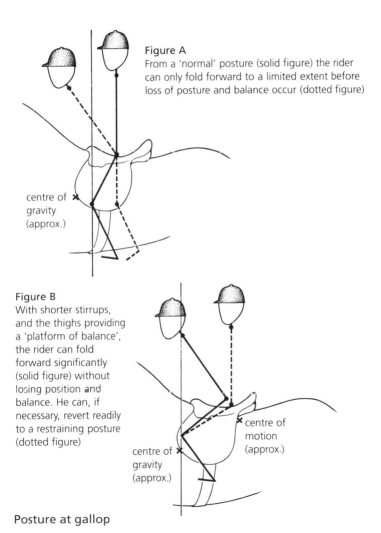

Figure A
From a 'normal' posture (solid figure) the rider can only fold forward to a limited extent before loss of posture and balance occur (dotted figure)

centre of gravity (approx.)

Figure B
With shorter stirrups, and the thighs providing a 'platform of balance', the rider can fold forward significantly (solid figure) without losing position and balance. He can, if necessary, revert readily to a restraining posture (dotted figure)

centre of gravity (approx.)

centre of motion (approx.)

Posture at gallop

'platform of balance' (represented by his seat) is not very wide. As long as the posture is upright, it is quite wide enough but, once the upper body is moved significantly in front of the vertical, the 'platform of balance' is too narrow to maintain the equilibrium. It will, instead, tend to act as a pivot, with the legs swinging backwards counter to the tilt of the upper body. (This point can be proved by sitting at halt without stirrups, and attempting to fold the upper body forwards as far as possible without losing balance or exerting undue grip with legs/thighs.)

What is needed, therefore, is a 'platform of balance' wide enough to support the degree of folding forward necessary to remain in harmony with the horse. This is produced by shortening the stirrup leathers. The result of shortening the leathers is that the angles of the knees and hips are closed and the thighs move forwards and upwards, adding to the width of the 'platform of balance'. The shorter the stirrups, the wider this platform will be, but very short stirrups can create problems of their own, and the idea is to shorten them sufficiently for the purpose without going to the extent of provoking these problems. The actual degree of shortening will depend upon the physique of horse and rider, the rider's intentions and the shape of the saddle (racing and jumping saddles being 'forward cut') so that their knee rolls can accommodate the changed leg position).

'Mechanically' speaking, the rider will be most secure if the stirrups are short enough for him to adopt his required upper body posture without his shoulder being in front of a vertical line through his knee. However, this is difficult to really check beforehand and, since we are thinking in terms of galloping riding school horses rather than race-riding, shortening the leathers three or four holes from the normal 'flatwork' length should suffice in most cases.

With the stirrups thus adjusted, the rider will be able to adopt a 'poised' posture, with the upper body folded forwards and the seat just clear of the saddle. The legs should automatically remain in position with the heels on the girth, and no attempt should be made to move them forwards or backwards, or to straighten them. The overall posture will be readily retained by the balance inherent in the posture, supplemented by light grip with the thighs.

The horse's head and neck move significantly at gallop, in a forward-down-back-up cycle, and the rider's hands and forearms must keep in harmony. It is important from the point of view of control, and the horse's balance, that the rein contact is not allowed to 'come and go'. It is also important that the rider is not tempted to take a dead hold/pull on the reins, since this will *not* enhance control, but merely provoke the horse into 'pulling' back.

If, then, the rider is in a 'poised' position, and is maintaining a responsive rein contact, he will be both in harmony with the horse and able to maintain sufficient control to keep the horse 'bowling along' at the chosen speed in normal circumstances. However, circumstances can arise during gallop which make it necessary to exercise prompt and effective restraint, beyond the normal process of asking the horse to gradually slacken pace. In addition to the possibility of the horse becoming overexcited, such circumstances may include sudden and unexpected changes in terrain/ground conditions, the possibility of a collision with a third party, etc. In such an event, the rider will have to alter his posture from one where the main emphasis is on allowing the horse to move freely forward, to one where the emphasis in on control. This is achieved by moving the upper body back to the vertical, so that the rider's weight is over the centre of motion. The seat may either be returned to the saddle or, if the horse has become very 'strong', it may be kept just above the saddle so that the rider can utilise the big muscles of thigh and back to effect restraint.

From such a posture, rein restraint is applied by keeping a firm, steady contact on one rein and repeatedly 'taking and releasing' the other in a measured manner, without snatching/jerking the reins, and without ever abandoning the rein contact. This method of restraint/stopping quickly should only be employed when it is necessary in terms of safety. Normally, the rider should slow the pace as gently as possible, keeping his legs against the horse's sides and gradually unfolding the upper body and using similar, but lighter rein aids to ease the horse back to the slower gaits.

The process of gradually unfolding the body emphasises that the rider need not necessarily adopt either a very 'forward' poised position or else a completely vertical posture; there are various phases between the two extremes, and, in practical situations, the rider will often wish to strike a compromise between placing his weight helpfully and exercising a modicum of restraint. This 'half speed' posture is also employed when riding in the open at a strong canter, when it will help keep the rider in harmony with movement which is less extreme than that of gallop. Before attempting to gallop, the rider should, in fact demonstrate his ability to control the horse fully in this strong canter, and practice in this gait will provide valuable experience for the rider who intends to graduate to jumping and various forms of riding cross-country.

Work at the strong canter will provide valuable experience for the rider who intends to graduate to riding cross-country.

▪ **The Aids**

The term 'aids' is used to describe the means by which the rider communicates with the horse, and also the specific signals given via these lines of communication. In order to be effective, the aids must:

1. Be inherently simple, in order that the horse is able to understand them fully.

2. Have direct, logical links with the horse's psychology, physiology and natural movement.

3. Be capable of application from the saddle, without disturbing the rider's posture or balance.

As lines of communication, it is important that the aids remain in constant 'contact' the whole time the horse is being actively ridden. This does not mean to say that they need to be continually giving specific, repetitive signals (this will, in fact, prove counter-productive), but the *means* of giving signals precisely as and when required must be there. An analogy is holding a telephone conversation; as long as the line is open the communicants can talk and listen as required but, if the receiver is replaced, the line becomes dead and communication is impossible.

When giving specific signals, all aids should be applied as lightly *as is effective*, and it is a sign of good riding/training that a horse gives progressively better responses to progressively lighter aids. However, the fundamental emphasis must be on effectiveness, with refinement following on. To define our terms, an effective aid is one which produces the desired response, and the lighter and more subtle it is, the better. An aid which produces an insufficient response must be considered ineffective, regardless of any theoretical 'correctness', while an aid which produces responses at variance with the rider's wishes must be considered inappropriate. This last category will include over-strong aids which may certainly have an effect, but one which is too dramatic to classify as a desired response.

The aids must, therefore, be evaluated upon their results, and the rider should be prepared to be flexible in his applications. While there are generally accepted principles for applying the aids for particular movements, horses are not machines, and there is no magic or push-button formula that will guarantee good results on each and every horse under all circumstances. If a specific aid application produces a good result from one horse, but does not do so from another, this may well indicate some deficiencies of training in the latter. However, if the rider persists in repeating *exactly* the same aid with the same unsatisfactory result, this indicates his own lack of understanding of what he is trying to achieve; his task is to find aids which elicit at least *some* measure of positive response. To this end, the rider must always take into consideration the mental and physical state of the horse being ridden, and any external factors (ground conditions, etc.) which may be influential.

In many instances, unsatisactory responses to the aids can be traced to rider error, and the rider must always be prepared to ask himself whether the horse understood, or was capable of doing, what he was asked. Very often, the honest rider will have to admit that his aids were confusing, contradictory, mistimed or over/under demanding. Such errors form part of the learning process, and are by no means confined to the 'novice' stages. Of course, when under instruction, the pupil will have the benefit of the teacher's observations and advice in such matters but, while he should obviously respect them, he should also be pre-

---

Remember that communication is a two-way process. Use the aids to tell the horse what you want him to do – but remember to 'listen' to what his responses are telling you.

The aids: there is no magic formula that will guarantee good results on each and every horse.

pared to think for himself, and try to evaluate his own riding. This combination of self-assessment with instruction will help to produce an active, effective horseman, rather than a 'robotic' rider who ceases to function the moment the instructor's attention is turned elsewhere.

We shall see in due course that the aids for specific movements are invariably applied in combinations, which must be harmonious and complementary. In the first instance, however, it will be useful to look at the individual aids, their main functions, and areas of influence.

LEGS The legs are used to initiate, maintain or increase forward movement, and also play a major role in producing and controlling lateral 'bend' and direction of travel.

As a means of communication, they must be kept operative by resting lightly but definitely against those parts of the horse's sides which they will touch naturally when the rider is in a correct posture. The rider should not make undue efforts to clamp the whole length of his legs against the horse, since the rounded shape of the horse's 'barrel' mitigates against this, and attempts to do so may result in a strained posture and too much 'dead' pressure on the horse. The phrase 'feeling the horse's hair with the legs' sums up the sensation the rider should be seeking. This is the starting point from which the rider can use his legs to give specific aids, but it also represents the minimum degree of leg contact which he should maintain. The legs should *never* be taken completely 'off' the horse, since to do so is to abandon a key line of communication and control. 'Legs off' *does* not mean 'stop' or 'slow down'; it means 'I am willing to become a mere passenger.'

From their position of light contact on, or just behind the girth, the legs can slide along the horse's flanks over an area reaching from the girth back to a vertical line through the centre of motion. Within this area, varying degrees of pressure can be applied to give specific signals. The pressure should be applied with the insides of the calves, feet or heels; turning the feet and legs 'toes outwards' will result in the postural problems already mentioned.

The degrees of pressure required to give effective aids will vary according to circumstance but, in general, the rider should be thinking in terms of 'squeezing', 'pressing' and 'nudging'; unnecessary harshness should be avoided. While there are (in my opinion) occasions when it is justifiable to apply aids in the form of a kick, these are few and far between, and never actually desirable. If the rider feels a need to habitually apply the aids in such a manner, this is indicative of technical or conceptual problems on his part, or severe deficiencies in the training or condition of the horse. Whatever the precise degree of pressure, it should only be applied to produce the required result; once the horse has responded, the leg(s) should resume their role of quiet communication. The process of continually 'nagging' at the horse with the heels is counter-productive; he will soon realise that there is no purposeful message behind these rather irritating 'signals', and thus start to pay less attention to both these, and other, leg aids.

The fundamental reasons for avoiding harsh or superfluous leg aids lie, therefore, not only in consideration for the horse, but also in maintaining the principle upon which the aids actually operate. This is the utilisation of the horse's natural response to stimuli; if pressure is applied to a particular point, his tendency is to move away from the source of pressure, or, by extension of the principle, to stop moving 'into' such pressure.

Thus, aids concerned with controlling bend and direction involve applying pressure to an appropriate point on one side of the horse, while the other leg remains quietly in communication (ready to act, if necessary, to maintain the level of forward movement). When the requirement is for the horse to move straight forwards, both legs are applied symmetrically and with equal pressure. Since the stimuli are equal on both sides, there is no logic in the horse's responding by moving sideways so, if he is to respond at all, he must move forwards or backwards. As his natural mode of progression is forwards, this is the most likely response. However, moving forwards is not the only possible response; the horse can either ignore the aids, or else move backwards. Lack of response, being contrary to the horse's nature, is only likely if he has learnt to ignore the aids through constant 'niggling', or is used to such heavy aids that anything lighter fails to register. Moving backwards is also, to some extent, unnatural, and suggests that something is discouraging the horse from moving forwards. However, if a horse does respond to a leg aid in this manner, the rider will be hard put to stop him, since he has no means of physically preventing backward movement except the use of further leg aids. This is why, in the early stages of training, it is of paramount importance that the horse's instinctive reactions are nurtured and reinforced, so that he learns to respond correctly to leg aids in general ('moving away from the leg') and aids to move straight forward in particular ('free forward movement').

Since the principles of basic training continue to apply in general riding, it follows that the rider should do nothing to encourage the horse to ignore, or react adversely to, these aids.

HANDS The hands, via reins and bit, communicate with the horse's mouth and, by extension, with his forehand. The functions of the hands are complementary to those of the legs; they provide a 'point of reference' at the front of the horse, into which he can be ridden, they meter out the forward movement, and they guide the forehand in unison with the directional aids/bend produced in the horse's body by the legs.

These functions are all dependent upon the rein contact, which must be retained in a manner 'acceptable' to the horse. The contact must not be abandoned unless the rider deliberate-

> Before you can begin to use your hands correctly, you must abandon any thought of the reins as a means of security. Without a reasonably secure posture, correct rein aids are impossible.

Rein contact must be retained in a manner which is acceptable to the horse, it must not be the cause of discomfort.

ly allows the horse a loose rein as a reward after work, or in order to assess the value of a schooling session. On the other hand, it must not be hardened to the extent that it induces any discomfort which the horse will try to resist or evade, and which constitutes a discouragement for him to move forwards from the leg aids. (Even in an emergency, where swift restraint is the overriding requirement, the rein aids should be applied intermittently, and not by sawing at the horse's mouth or taking a dead pull with both reins, since these actions will encourage resistance rather than submission.)

Since we are considering horses which are suitable for novice pupils to learn on, I am making the assumption that they will be trained to a level whereby they *are* willing to accept a reasonable rein contact, but it may be instructive to look very briefly at how this is done, on the grounds that an understanding of the training principle will help in general riding. In the early stages of training, the horse is first taught to accept the presence of a bit in his mouth, and encouraged to 'mouth' (play with) it, to increase familiarisation and produce saliva, which helps lubricate the bit. He is then taught to accept a light contact on the bit without resistance, and this is achieved by establishing a practical length of rein and riding the horse forward into a 'soft' contact. This contact is never hardened by the rider, but, if the horse resists, the rider does not 'surrender' the rein, he maintains the contact and pushes the horse forward more firmly with the legs, at the same time gently vibrating (*not* sawing) the bit in the horse's mouth, until the horse responds by relaxing his jaw. As soon as he does so, the rider offers a soft, still contact. After a while, in addition to accepting the bit, the horse will start to expect the contact so that, if the rider eases/releases it, he will stretch forward and down 'seeking the bit'. When this stage is reached, it is apparent that the horse is prepared to accept the bit as a 'point of reference' for his forehand, and that he will be willing to listen to rein aids which involve minor changes of rein contact produced by various actions of the rider's wrists and fingers.

The value of the rein contact as a 'point of reference' which the horse will recognise is, then, that it allows the rider to instigate forward movement which he can influence and control with minimal force and to maximum effect. If he had no contact with the front of the horse, or a contact which the horse did not acknowledge, he would obviously have minimal control over the forward movement. If he had a contact which was unacceptably harsh, then the horse would not readily move forward and/or would 'fight' for his head.

The idea of the horse not moving readily forward may seem superficially attractive when the subject of slowing or stopping is considered. However, a review of the horse's way of movement

Contact with the horse's mouth should not be abandoned unless you are purposely giving him a chance to relax and stretch his neck.

will show that this is false logic. We have established that a horse moving actively 'from behind' in a rounded, balanced outline will be best able to control his own movements, and thus respond correctly to the wishes of the rider, and this fact applies to *all* movements, including changing gait, slowing down and stopping. If, therefore, this balance and outline are destroyed or disturbed, this will make it *harder* for the horse to respond to the rider's signals.

Furthermore, an examination of the situation suggests that there is no requirement to stop the horse 'going forward'. If, for instance, the rider wishes to change gait from trot to walk, his actual requirement is for the horse to *keep going forward*, but in a different gait. Similarly, if the horse is moving too fast in the chosen gait, then the requirement is for him to *keep going forward*, but in a more measured manner. The factual exception to this principle is when halting, in which case, by definition, the horse must stop. Even so, the principle still pertains in that the horse must go *forward* into halt, in order to halt correctly and in a manner from which he can readily resume movement when required.

This brings us to the question of the precise role and function of the hands in controlling forward movement without affecting the horse's *willingness* to move forwards. The answer lies in the horse's acceptance of the contact, and his consequent preparedness to respond to sensitive variations in its degree. From the basic light but firm hold of the reins, the rider can either 'soften' the contact by opening the angles of wrist and fingers, or else increase it by closing the angles. The extent of these movements is sufficient for a responsive horse to 'take note', but the degree by which the contact can be increased in this manner should not cause any discomfort. The horse is, therefore, getting an acceptable signal to 'steady' his front end.

However, given in isolation, this signal is still the equivalent of 'applying the front brake only', and the mechanical consequences of doing this are broadly the same on a horse as on a powered vehicle. What is required, therefore, is a corresponding signal to the 'back end' which, as we have seen, cannot be given by taking the legs 'off' the horse. If a signal is to be given then, the only alternative is to *apply* the legs. This may sound a complete contradiction, the argument being that 'the back end is being asked to go forward, and the front end to slow/stop'. However, performed correctly, this combination of aids forms the basis of all controls of forward movement. The explanation of this is that a gentle leg aid, applied fractionally before the rein aid, invites the horse to move forwards 'into' the containing contact. The rider is saying 'keep going forwards, but in a more controlled fashion'. As with the other aids, as soon as the horse has responded, the contact must be eased back to its 'normal' degree so that the rider does not get into the position of a sustained application of both 'accelerator' and 'brake'.

The action of the hands when the rider wishes to increase forward movement is dependent upon his specific requirements. Since the horse should accept the 'normal' degree of contact at all times, it is not automatically essential to lighten it, although many horses (especially the less highly trained) appreciate being 'offered' a way forward. However, when the rider's requirements involve a lengthening of the horse's outline (as is associated with lengthened strides), his hands must act to accommodate the lengthening of the head and neck, otherwise the net effect will be to *increase* the contact.

As directional aids, the hands simply 'ask' the horse to look in the required direction of travel. This is achieved by 'opening' the hand on the other side to which the horse must move. For instance, if the rider wishes to circle to the left, he moves his left hand a little in that direction. As with all control of movement,

Even in the rush and tumble of a hunt these riders are not pulling their horses heads round with their inside hands.

this aid must be given in conjunction with the appropriate leg aids, the aim being not merely to 'steer' the front end of the horse, but to place his whole body on an arc of the required size and direction. By the same token, the action of the hand must not be in any way backwards, since this will merely wrench the horse's head and neck round in a manner and to an extent that the rest of his body cannot, and is not required, to follow. In fact, even moving the hand directly sideways will effectively increase the rein contact unless the horse responds by instantaneous lateral flexion of his neck. Since this is a potential source of resistance and loss of activity, it can, in many instances, be useful to give the rein aid by moving the hand sideways and slightly forward, thus 'offering' the horse a direction in which to move.

SEAT We have seen that, by acting as a stabiliser and shock absorber, the seat allows the other aids to be applied to optimum effect, and establishing it in this role is the first priority. However, once a balanced, 'adhesive' seat has been established, the rider will discover that it can, in itself, act as a highly versatile aid for stimulating and controlling movement; a role which will become increasingly influential as the rider progresses.

Communication through the seat results simply from sitting in the saddle, but it is the ability to do so without erratic or random shifts of weight which provides the basis for giving specific signals. Since the applications of the seat aids are perhaps less straightforward in concept than those of legs and hands, it may be an advantage if the first practical applications are attempted in a lesson where they are given special emphasis or, better still, on the lunge, where their effects can be explored in isolation.

There are two main ways in which the rider can give aids with the seat; by bracing the lower back (lumbar vertebrae) and by varying weight distribution. With increasing experience, these aids will be employed to varying degrees and, at times, almost

This dressage rider is using legs, seat and hands combined to produce the spectacular flying change movement.

subconsciously, in conjunction with other aids. However, for our purposes, the broad principles can be considered as follows:

1. Bracing the back: the mechanical influence of this aid results from the position of the rider's spine pretty much vertically over the horse's centre of motion, and his consequent ability to use his weight to influence the horse's locomotion. Bracing the lower back (beyond the normal erect posture) will result in a forward driving effect, which is apparent even when sitting on a hard chair. This effect can be used in conjunction with, and supplementary to, the leg aids. Using 'seat and legs'

> Many riders who consider themselves beyond the novice stage
> have no concept of the seat as an aid. Riding without using the
> seat is like flying an aeroplane with one wing. Develop a determi-
> nation to find out how you can use your seat.

whilst 'allowing' the horse forward with the hands, will produce extra forward movement: the same 'seat and leg' aids
into a 'containing' rein contact will produce a stronger and
more effective 'steadying' aid than would be produced by the
legs alone. The 'restraining posture', employed if necessary at
the faster gaits, is an adaptation of this latter principle; even
if the rider's seat remains out of the saddle, he is using the
influence of back and legs to effect restraint.

However, use of the seat and back in this manner is not
confined to 'strong' aids and, in common with all aid applications, the seat should be used as lightly as is practical – the
consequence of misapplied thrusting movements has already
been mentioned in connection with canter. With practice, the
rider will find that quite slight bracing of the back can be
effective in 'containing' a keen horse who is anticipating
quickening or changing gait, and also in encouraging more
activity in the hindquarters when seeking a more 'rounded'
outline.

2. Varying weight distribution: since we have established that
instability and crookedness constitute postural errors, it is
important to understand that these uses of the seat do not
constitute, and are not excuses for, sitting incorrectly. They
are subtle uses of an established seat which can be employed
to good effect when the rider reaches the stage of thinking
mainly in terms of improving the horse's way of going.

From a 'normal' starting point, where the weight of the
seat is spread pretty evenly through thighs and buttocks, it is
possible to redistribute the weight in the following ways:

a. Deepening the seat, by lightening the burden on the thighs, and increasing the burden on the buttocks. This is, to a large extent, a product of bracing the back, and tends to increase the 'driving' effect of the seat.

b. Lightening the seat, by increasing the burden on the thighs, and decreasing that on the buttocks. A simple, if extreme, example of this is seen in rising trot. The tendency is to decrease the 'driving' effect of the seat, and this can be useful when trying to 'settle' rather than 'contain' keen or highly-strung horses.

c. Slight alterations in weight distribution between the seat-bones. This can help to supplement other directional aids, but should not be overdone – i.e. the rider should not habitually lean in the direction in which he wants to go.

VOICE The tone of voice can be used to soothe, encourage, admonish or reprimand the horse. As with the other aids, the voice should be used sparingly and to a purpose. Although horses

The voice can be an effective aid!

respond primarily to tone of voice, there is no doubt that they can learn to understand (associate) specific words. This can be very useful for trainers working a horse on the lunge, but causes complications in the riding school when knowing old horses react to the instructor's command rather than the rider's aids!

It is interesting to note that, although the voice is, self-evidently, a 'natural' aid, its use in dressage competitions is penalised.

■ 'Artificial' Aids

The aids already described, being uses of the rider's own body, are usually referred to as 'natural' aids. The term 'artificial' aids is used to describe devices (other than the saddle and standard types of bridle) intended to reinforce/supplement the natural aids.

Although they sometimes have legitimate and useful applications, the artificial aids should be employed with discretion and only in conjunction with, never instead of, the natural aids they are intended to support. It is obvious that the more effectively the natural aids can be applied, the less need there will be for recourse to the artificial ones. The main aids are:

THE WHIP This is usually carried in the rider's 'inside' hand when in the arena, and the 'outside' (normally the right) hand when on the road. It should be held handle uppermost, resting lightly across the fingers on the 'outside' of the rein – that is, not between the rein and the hand.

Although the whip can be used as a means of punishing genuine disobedience, its main function is as an extra stimulus to support the leg aids. In the early stages of training, when the horse is being taught to move forwards from leg pressure, the whip may be applied lightly just behind the leg, at the same time as the leg aid is given. The extra stimulus reinforces the leg aid,

The whip is usually carried in the rider's inside hand when in the arena.

and the horse learns to associate the pressure of the legs alone with the dual effect of both leg and whip, and thus responds more readily to the aids.

This principle holds good beyond the stage of basic training; if, in due course, the horse ceases to respond readily to the leg aids, the whip can be reintroduced to 'wake him up', thus preventing any tendency for the rider to resort to more and stronger leg aids.

Experienced riders engaged in training and schooling horses usually employ a long schooling whip. In educated hands, this can prove very effective, but its length, and the fact that it is applied with the 'whip hand' still holding the rein, can render its use by an inexperienced rider clumsy and counter-productive. Any backward movement of the hand as the whip is applied will result in the horse being pulled in the mouth at the very moment he is being given a signal to go forward. Therefore, until the rider is certain that he has full control over his hands, it is more practical to carry a shorter whip, which is used after taking both reins in one hand.

If the whip is to be used as an instrument of punishment, it should be reversed (thong uppermost) from the carrying position, and applied smartly and accurately to the horse's quarters. In order that the horse may associate the punishment with the disobedience he must be hit immediately after disobeying; delayed punishment is totally useless, and more indicative of revenge than admonishment. Further to this point, the rider should only punish the horse if he is totally convinced that he has exhibited wilful disobedience to a reasonable and readily understood command. If there is any cause to suspect that the horse is frightened or confused, then punishment is altogether inappropriate. This principle applies to all riders, but is especially important for novices, who may not have the experience to evaluate fully the circumstances of a particular incident.

SPURS The type of spurs properly used in equitation are short and blunt, and have nothing in common with the horrific devices beloved of the makers of Westerns. However, they do provide a more obvious and concentrated stimulus than a normal leg aid applied with the same pressure, and this is the principle upon which they operate. Spurs have two legitimate uses:

1. Since they heighten the effect of a leg aid, they can be employed to give very subtle but still effective aids. (It is for this reason that they are worn by dressage exponents, although it is hard to understand why it should be *compulsory* to wear them in the higher levels of competition.)

2. To reinforce the leg aids during remedial schooling of a horse who has 'stopped listening' to the leg (a similar role to that of the whip).

If spurs are worn and used correctly, the rider has the option of giving leg aids with or without spur support as required. However, this pre-supposes that he has full control of his leg position and aid applications, and that he understands fully the principles involved. Given these criteria, and the nature of the spurs themselves, it will be apparent that their use by an inexperienced rider is inappropriate at best, and may be potentially dangerous.

OTHER DEVICES This category includes abnormal types of bits, nosebands, and various forms of running and check reins designed to use leverage to artificially impose the rider's will upon the horse's outline and progression. Their use should be totally unnecessary on any horse suitable for riding school clients, who should consider them only as a warning sign. Many of these devices are unfortunately popular at the present time, and they are most commonly used by riders who view them as a short-cut and/or substitute for skill.

■ Applying the Aids

Correct and effective use of the aids to produce and control movement is what riding is all about, a fact summed up to perfection in the maxim 'ride your horse forward and hold it straight' (Gustave Steinbrecht). The two criteria of this sentence lie at the root of all aid applications, and it may be instructive to consider their impact before looking at the aids for various movements.

RIDING FORWARDS We have already examined the reasons for encouraging forward movement, and touched upon the principle of riding 'forward' at all times. In order to follow this principle through, it is necessary to apply all combinations of aids 'from the back to the front'; in other words, to ride from the seat and legs 'into' the hands. This principle applies even to movements started from halt, where the legs must stimulate a *desire* for forward movement, even if the requirement is to turn 'on the spot' (turn on the forehand). The logic behind this is that, if the horse is to move, he must always want to move forwards – an intention which can be re-directed as required by correct use of the aids.

Mention of the horse 'wanting' to move forward brings us to the principle of impulsion, a characteristic complementary to free forward movement. Whereas free forward movement might be defined as the horse being agreeable to moving forward, impulsion is often defined as a *desire* to do so, in much the same way as a person who is happy in their work might want to 'get on with the job'. This characteristic is to be nurtured and encouraged since, not only does it suggest an enthusiasm on the horse's part, it also makes the rider's job easier. If the horse is willing to move forwards, he will do so from lighter and less frequent aids, and the rider will be able to concentrate his mental and physical energies in other directions. However, the rider must learn to distinguish between impulsion, where the horse steps willingly forward 'from behind', and 'hurrying' or 'running', where the horse goes relatively fast, but by taking quick, short 'scuttling' steps.

> The fundamental reason for sitting on a horse is to be carried somewhere. It is a stark truth that a rider who does not want the horse to move forwards would be better off sitting on a chair. From an early stage, study to encourage and welcome forward movement in the horse.

This latter is linked to lack of balance (from various causes), and may also be a result of the horse 'evading' the aids. An example of this is the crafty old school horse who, when it is his turn to move round the arena to the rear of the 'ride', puts his head down and scampers off, cutting the corners so that he can finish the job while doing as little real work as possible. In all instances, this sort of movement is characterised by the horse tipping onto his forehand and 'leaning' on the rider's hands. The basic means of overcoming this, re-balancing the horse and producing more activity, is to ride a half-halt, or series of half-halts. As the name suggests, there are major similarities between the aids for this movement and those to halt, or change 'down' a gait. The rider braces his back, closes his legs more firmly against the horse's sides, and asks him to step forward into a 'containing' rein contact. However, after the horse has responded to the seat and legs by stepping more under himself, but before he has fully responded to the rein aid, the rider softens the contact and allows the forward movement.

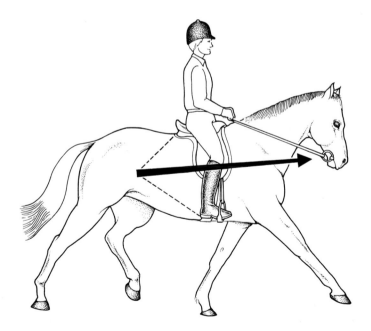

Applying the aids effectively. Rider's seat and legs encourage active movement 'from behind'. Hands maintain an 'acceptable' contact, controlling, but not stifling the forward movment. The overall effect is of great impulsion coupled with willing obedience.

Ridden correctly, the half-halt balances the horse, 'lightens' his forehand and makes him more attentive. It is thus invaluable at any time when there is a need to improve the horse's movement.

With practise, it is possible to ride very subtle half-halts, which produce the required effects without taking the horse 'halfway' to actually halting.

STRAIGHTNESS In equestrian terminology 'straightness' can mean rather more than moving in a straight line. It includes the idea of the horse's hind feet following in the tracks of his forefeet, whether going straight forward or travelling on a circle. At a more advanced level, it can mean even more than this; in 'lateral' movements, where the hind and forefeet follow different tracks, it can imply that the horse maintains the required direction (forward and sideways), with his hind and forefeet continuing to move parallel to each other. In short, 'straightness' means that the whole horse continues to move accurately in the prescribed direction.

Straightness is a desirable characteristic not only in terms of accurate riding, but because it *promotes* accuracy by virtue of the 'straight' horse being better balanced and more controllable. Unfortunately, most horses are not naturally 'straight'; they are often slightly asymmetrical in physique (just like humans) and/or tend to be either 'left' or 'right' handed. These characteristics can be aggravated by incorrect training, sometimes to the extent that a horse becomes completely 'one-sided'. Although such cases should not be the concern of the novice pupil, he should be aware of the lesser problems, so that he can understand the need to ride the horse equally 'on both reins', and appreciate why some horses are noticeably stiffer on one side than the other, and harder to ride in that direction.

However, assuming that the horse is sufficiently well-trained to go reasonably straight if given the chance, the rider must be careful that his own actions do not induce loss of straightness. He should, therefore, avoid errors which will cause this directly (sitting lop-sided, 'hanging on' to one rein, etc.), and also those which may provoke loss of straightness by frustrating, rather than redirecting, the horse's desire to go forwards (for instance, a crooked halt caused by pulling on the reins and creating a 'front brake skid' effect).

Following on from this latter point, it is worth noting that the more actively a horse is encouraged/allowed to move forwards (without rushing), the 'straighter' he is likely to be. This is because:

1. The forward movement will help balance the horse, and counter the effects of any conformation defects.

2. It will mean, by definition, that the rider is not provoking crookedness.

3. Active forward movement will help keep the horse attentive, thereby discouraging any crookedness which might arise from disobedience or lack of concentration on his part.

Bearing these principles in mind, let us now look at the aids for specific movements.

MOVING IN A STRAIGHT LINE Once the horse is moving forwards in the desired manner, the rider should retain an erect, perpendicular posture, light, symmetrical communication with both legs, and an 'acceptable' contact with both reins.

MOVING ON A CIRCLE To ride a circle well, it is important to have a clear mental picture of the size and shape of the figure. The latter requirement may seem over-obvious, but many odd-shaped figures are ridden by people who know perfectly well that a circle is round.

Imagining that the route is marked out with a white line, or has to be ridden along tracks, can help establish the mental image. The first quarter of the circle is most important because, if correct bend and rhythm are established, the rider will merely have to 'keep going' to produce a good figure. If, however, the first quarter is incorrect, then the rider is likely to spend the rest of the time 'looking for' the circle.

Since it is more difficult for a horse to move on a circle than in a straight line, the rider should be ready to ask for a little more activity as he moves into the figure, in order that the horse retains his tempo. He should, however, be careful to ask the horse to step more actively 'into' the rein contact, and must avoid 'throwing the reins' at him and 'chasing' him into a longer outline; actions which will only result in loss of balance.

The horse should be introduced to the circle by 'offering' a change of direction with the inside rein (that on the side to which he is to circle), while the rider's outside leg slides quietly back behind the girth to 'contain' the natural tendency for the horse to swing his quarters out. It is important that the outside leg is not 'clamped' or 'banged' against the horse's side, since this may be interpreted as a crude aid to canter.

A slight bracing of the back will help encourage forward movement, and also help to keep the rider sitting upright and square to the axis. This posture must be maintained, and the rider should not endeavour to influence the horse by leaning or twisting in either direction, since such actions will merely disturb his balance.

There is a commonly-quoted principle that, on a circle, the 'outside rein controls the speed, and the inside rein controls the bend'. While this is a broadly correct description of the functions of the reins in *conjunction with the other aids*, it is important

---

To maintain activity and rhythm on a circle, think 'First we go forwards, then we go round'.

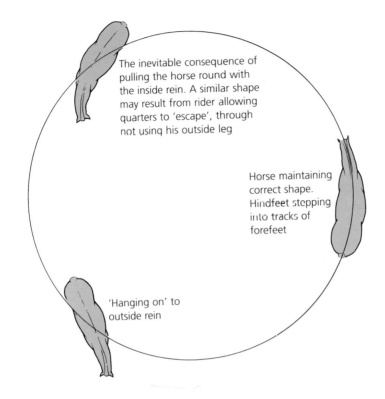

The inevitable consequence of pulling the horse round with the inside rein. A similar shape may result from rider allowing quarters to 'escape', through not using his outside leg

Horse maintaining correct shape. Hindfeet stepping into tracks of forefeet

'Hanging on' to outside rein

Correct and incorrect movement on a circle

that it is understood in this light, and is not interpreted as meaning that this is the sole function of the reins, and of the reins alone.

In fact, the two commonest errors when riding circles stem from misuse of the reins. Perhaps the most prevalent consists of trying to pull the horse round the circle with the inside rein. While this is, to some extent, understandable as an instinctive action, the result is to create too much lateral bend of the head and neck only, and to encourage the hindquarters to swing outside the line of the circle. The rider who finds himself tempted

Work on a circle.

into this effort should remember the requirement to 'offer' the horse a direction, and ride the whole horse, rather than merely try to 'steer' the front end.

The 'opposite' error results from trying to 'hold' a horse out on the circle with the outside rein, or, alternatively, employing the rein in isolation to 'check' a horse who is hurrying. The consequence of pulling/hanging onto the outside rein is that the horse becomes 'bent' in the wrong direction, and his quarters swing inside the line of the circle, thus destroying the shape. The remedy for the horse who is trying to 'hang in' from the circle is not to 'pull' him out, but rather firstly, to ride him more forwards, and then to use the inside leg to 'push' him out. In the case of the horse who is 'hurrying', he should be checked and re-balanced by a correctly-ridden half-halt, as if he were travelling in a straight line.

▪ Turning

The most common way of changing direction on horseback is simply by riding part of an appropriately sized circle. In order to ride an accurate turn, it follows that the principles pertaining to full circles are adhered to. The most frequent use of such turns in the arena is when riding through corners and, since these require only a quarter circle, it is important that the shape is not lost through allowing the horse to 'anticipate' the turn and cut the corner.

A corner properly ridden at trot.

The size of the part circle ridden will depend upon size and training of the horse, skill of the rider, ground conditions, and the gait at which the turn is performed. In circumstances where there is no restriction on space, it is sensible to ride wide turns, which are easier for both horse and rider. In the (standard) arena, where the largest circle possible is 20 m (66 ft) diameter, it follows that all turns must form parts of circles this size or smaller. At an early stage, it is better to concentrate on riding wide turns correctly, but, as the rider's skill increases, he can start to ask for small part circles.

There are no hard and fast rules concerning the dimensions of turns, but, as a rough guide, a reasonably proficient rider on a moderately well trained horse should be able to perform 90 degree turns based on circles of the following diameters:

at walk	6–8 m (19-26 ft)
at trot	10 m (33 ft)
at canter	15 m (50 ft)

The other means of turning; on the forehand, on the haunches and on the centre have already been described from the horse's point of view. The aids are:

TURN ON THE FOREHAND This movement must be started at a point sufficiently far from the arena perimeter to permit the turn to be made. The horse should be ridden forwards into a correct halt. The rider moves his leg on the side to which the horse is to turn a little behind the girth, and 'asks' for a slight lateral flexion of head and neck in the direction of the proposed turn. He then

applies sufficient pressure with the leg behind the girth to push the quarters *away* from the direction of the turn, so that the horse pivots on his 'inside' foreleg until facing in the required direction. The rider's other leg retains communication on the girth to counteract any tendency to step backwards, while the hands retain sufficient contact to prevent the horse from stepping forwards. (Of the two, stepping backwards is much the more serious error.)

Throughout the turn, the rider should remain upright, avoiding any tendency to

A corner properly ridden at canter.

lean in the direction of the turn. If the horse anticipates the turn and tries to hurry it, the leg aid should be suitably softened; if, however, the horse is reluctant to turn, the leg should be applied more firmly, but the rider should 'ask' for one step at a time, and not attempt to force the horse round with one mighty heave. Under no circumstances should any attempt be made to pull the horse round with the inside rein. As soon as the turn has been completed, the horse should be ridden actively forwards.

TURN ON THE HAUNCHES This turn should only be attempted from walk until such time as the rider has considerable experience, and is riding a well-trained, well-balanced horse. Even at walk, it is pointless to attempt the movement unless the gait is active, and the horse is 'between leg and hand'. It may assist in performing the turn if is preceded by a gentle half-halt, to help balance the horse and 'lighten' his forehand.

To perform the turn, the rider's leg on the side towards which the turn is to be made remains on the girth, gently encouraging the horse to think 'forward', and the hand on the same side 'opens' (not pulls) the rein significantly, leading the horse round the pivot of the inside hind leg. The rider's other leg slides back behind the girth to prevent the quarters from swinging out. It is most important that the hand 'leads' the horse round, and does not pull a lateral bend into head and neck, which will make swinging of the quarters inevitable.

Early attempts at this turn, for either horse or rider, will usually result in the horse describing a small circle with the inside hind foot, rather than actually pivoting on it. So long as the turn is otherwise satisfactory, and the rhythm is maintained, this can be considered acceptable – although the turn should become more accurate with practice.

TURN ON THE CENTRE The fact that this turn has limited practical applications on the ridden horse, and is executed in a manner rather readily associated with 'pulling the horse round on the spot', result in it being ignored by many instructors. Although they may have a good case, the movement is a legitimate way of turning, if performed correctly.

The turn on the centre can only be made from an active walk and, as with the turn on the haunches, the more balanced and responsive the horse, the better. To perform the turn, the rider's leg on the side away from the direction of turn remains on the girth, while the other 'inside' leg moves backwards as far as practical. The inside leg then pushes the quarters away from the direction of the turn, at the same time as the inside rein leads the forehand into the turn. Applied in correct combination, these aids will result in the horse pivoting in a united fashion round a central point.

▪ Transitions

Now that we have looked at the requirements for movement in general, we can examine how the individual gaits are produced and, since one gait will be instigated from another, this brings us to the topic of transitions.

Transitions are simply changes of gait, but they can be either 'progressive' or 'direct'. Progressive transitions are those which go 'through the gaits', for instance, to move from walk into canter, the rider would first ask for a few strides of trot, and then change gait from trot to canter. In a direct transition, the horse would be asked to move straight from walk into canter. There is no real difference in principle between the aids for progressive and direct transitions but, in order to perform the latter correctly, the horse *must* be moving actively and attentively, and the rider must have the experience, ability and confidence to apply the aids effectively, but without harshness or 'desperation'. (These requirements are obviously desirable for all transitions, but they are essential if the rider intends to 'miss a gait'.) For this

> Just as you would wish to change gear smoothly in your car in order to retain full control, work towards smooth transitions from the horse.

reason, and in the interest of simplicity, riders are taught progressive transitions first, it is these we shall concentrate upon.

However, before looking at individual transitions, it is worth considering the three phases which apply to all. These are:

1. Prepare. Ensure that the horse is moving actively in the present gait, and that he is 'straight' (i.e. physically straight if on a straight line, and correctly 'bent' if on a circle). If he is inactive, crooked or inattentive when asked for the transition, these faults will be reflected both in the transition itself and the ensuing gait. The rider should also prepare himself by checking his own posture, and having a clear idea of when and where he wishes to change gait.

2. Ask. Apply the appropriate aids clearly and without fuss.

3. Allow. Permit the horse to oblige. That is to say, do not do anything which will restrict/unbalance/inhibit his attempts to do so.

In addition to these phases being applicable to each and every transition, there are also factors common to all transitions 'up' (to a 'faster' gait), and to all transitions 'down' (to a 'slower' gait). This is hardly surprising since, in both cases, the aid is basically saying 'change to the next gait'; the purpose of any aid variations being simply to accommodate the different characteristics of the gaits. Bearing these points in mind, the aids for transitions 'up' are as follows:

HALT TO WALK Squeeze horse's sides with both legs evenly, slightly 'soften' rein contact to accommodate initial lengthening of horse's outline.

WALK TO TROT Apply leg aids as above, lighten the contact fractionally. Because of the differing gait characteristics between walk and trot, it may sometimes be necessary, once the gait is established, to shorten the reins a little in order to retain sufficient contact. If this becomes habitual, however, it may indicate that there is too little contact in walk. Should the rider wish to 'rise' to the trot, he should not do so until the gait is established.

TROT TO CANTER A pre-requisite is that the rider is sitting to the trot. In the early stages, it is easier to ask for canter in a corner of the arena, or when coming off a circle, since the horse should be 'bent' in the direction in which he is to canter, and it will be easier for him to 'lead' with the correct leg. If the transition is requested on the straight, it can help to 'feel' gently (but not pull) on the inside rein. The rider should slide his outside leg back a little behind the girth, and squeeze with both legs; the outer a little more firmly. The application of the outside leg is initially to encourage the correct hind leg to instigate the canter – if the rider wishes to circle, the leg should remain in place to 'contain' the horse's quarters. Common mistakes when asking for canter are 'hurrying' the horse in trot, and 'throwing the reins at him', both of which merely unbalance him onto the forehand, and make the transitions more difficult.

CANTER TO GALLOP Retain control at canter. Apply leg aids to ask for measured quickening. 'Allow' horse to lengthen outline but under no circumstances abandon rein contact. Fold gradually into appropriate 'poised' posture: do not adopt this posture in advance of the horse's movement.

In all these transitions, the leg aid should be a definite (although not necessarily firm) squeeze of short duration; once the horse has responded, the legs should resume their role of quiet

This rider has asked her horse to increase speed but has abandoned rein contact.

communication until the rider wishes to change/vary the gait or direction.

If the horse does not respond to the first aid, the rider should not resort to a general 'jamming on' of the aid, nor should he belabour the horse's sides with his heels; he should simply ask again, a little more firmly. If there is still no response, and he is satisfied that he himself is not preventing the horse from obeying, he should reinforce the next aid with the whip. (When asking for canter, it is sensible to change the whip into the outside hand, so that it is reinforcing the aid to establish the correct 'lead'.)

The more experienced rider, who is less likely to be interfering with the horse's response, may choose to use the whip and leg at the *second* time of asking.

The aids for transitions 'down' are all substantially the same, and are made by using the seat and legs to move the horse 'into' a 'containing' contact, as already described. It will assist the rider's understanding of both theory and practice of downward transitions if, in the early stages, some time is spent upon the following exercise.

The horse is ridden at 'free' walk, on quite a long rein and light contact. At intervals, the rider braces his back, thinks of sitting 'deep' into the saddle, and *thinks* of stopping his body and hands from moving forwards. (He should only think of stopping – he must not lean backwards or pull on the reins.) Although these actions may not produce a perfectly correct, 'square' halt, they should definitely result in the horse stopping, and will thus provide valuable evidence of the need to ride forward (the seat and back aid) in downward transitions, and prove that there is no need to pull back on the reins. Points relevant to specific changes of gait are:

GALLOP TO CANTER In all normal circumstances, this change of gait should be gradual, with the horse being 'eased', not 'pulled up'. If the horse is still keen to gallop, the aids will need to be stronger than, for instance, those given for trot to walk. However, the principle pertains that they should be just strong enough to be effective.

CANTER TO TROT In this transition, it is especially important to observe the principles and sequence of the aid applications. Any tendency to tip forward and pull on the reins will result in the horse 'falling' onto the forehand, and performing a scurrying trot which will bounce the rider up and down in the saddle. Being forced to 'rise' to the trot after a downward transition is an indication that the transition itself was faulty.

TROT TO WALK Should be performed from sitting trot.

In this transition the rider has too strong a rein contact and is not sitting down.

WALK TO HALT It is easy to halt, but a good deal less easy to halt correctly; a fact highlighted by the stationary 'evidence' of a poor transition. In dressage tests, etc., the requirements for halt are more precise than those for other transitions, and any rider with competitive ambitions (or who just wants to 'get it right') would do well to practise this transition.

▪ Gait variants

In the early stages, the rider should only be expected to establish reasonably active movement, that is to say 'free' walk and 'working' trot and canter. However, as he progresses, the principles of producing lengthened strides will be introduced. The basic aids for lengthening are to brace the lower back, apply fairly light but sustained leg pressure a little behind the girth, and allow the horse to lengthen his outline without feeling any hardening of rein contact.

While an average rider on a reasonably well-trained horse may expect to produce reasonable lengthening with a little practice, true 'collection' is a rather different matter. Pre-requisites are a highly-trained, responsive, well-muscled horse and a rider with the skill and experience to utilise these assets. In true collection, the horse must show great impulsion in response to the rider's aids, but also listen to the gentlest restraint of a light rein contact, and convert his energy not into long strides, but short, powerful, elevated steps. The first 'feel' that a rider is likely to get of this sort of movement is when receiving a correct response to a half-halt, but it is unlikely that the average school horse will be able to produce true, sustained collection even for an expert rider. The reader should, therefore, be wary of the term being used (as it frequently is) to desribe what is merely slow, inactive movement.

▪ Rein Back

Although this movement has practical applications, it is used in the school as an exercise in correct use of the aids by the rider, and obedience by the horse. Since the actual backward movement is at odds with the principle of encouraging forward movement at all times, rein back should be performed sparingly, and always preceded and followed by period of active forward work. It is, in fact, pointless to attempt the movement on a horse who is inactive, inattentive or in a 'hollow' outline.

In the early stages, the rein back should be ridden via a short, but distinct halt. The halt is produced in the usual manner, but,

> *Do not* conduct your own experiments in rein back by pulling on the reins – wait to learn the movement correctly under instruction.

A fair halt: the minimum required before attempting rein back.

once it is established, the rider does not 'ease' the aids, but continues to use his seat and legs to push the horse into still hands. He is, therefore, asking the horse for movement, but not allowing him to move forwards, so the only way in which he can respond is by moving backwards. Early attempts for horse or rider should consist of only a couple of steps, and these should be steady and regular; the horse must not be encouraged or allowed to 'run' backwards. The movement should be straight, and any crookedness will reflect crookedness at halt, uneven aids, or resistance/stiffness in the horse.

▪ Lateral Movements

'Lateral' movement occurs when, instead of following the tracks of the forefeet with the hind feet, the horse is intentionally asked to step both forwards and across himself, so that he moves forwards and sideways simultaneously. Basic lateral work is used to supple the horse in training, but, to be performed well, it also requires (especially in the more advanced movements) a high degree of suppleness and balance in the horse, and commensurate skill in the rider.

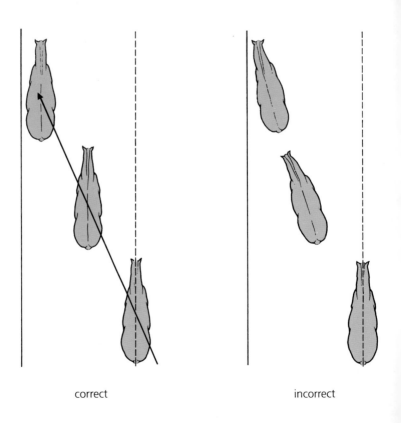

correct   incorrect

Leg-yielding

However, although the niceties of the individual movements will not be of practical concern to the novice rider, the basic principles behind the aids are far from mysterious, and a good instructor is likely to introduce pupils to these principles once a reasonable degree of general proficiency has been attained.

The turn on the forehand described previously is, essentially, a lateral movement but, this aside, the first lateral movement to which the novice is introduced will usually be 'leg-yielding'. The most common way of riding this movement is to turn down the inside track, 2 to 3 m (6–10 ft) 'inside' the arena perimeter, and then, keeping the outside leg lightly on the girth, apply stronger pressure with the inside leg, encouraging the horse to step forward and slightly sideways until he reaches the perimeter. When performing this movement, it is essential to remain erect and 'push' with the inside leg; leaning away from the direction of movement ('pushing' with the upper body) or pulling on the outside rein will not produce the required response. It is also important that the horse is ridden primarily forward, and sideways secondly, and that he is not allowed to just 'fall out' to the arena wall. In the early stages, the instructor will usually stand at the far end of the school, and evaluate the effect of the pupils' aids but, with a little practice, the rider will learn to feel whether or not the horse is responding correctly by stepping 'across' himself.

Leg-yielding is, essentially, a utility movement, the chief aim of which (from the rider's point of view) is to establish co-ordination of the aids. Once this has been achieved, the rider will be better equipped for an introduction to more advanced (and, ultimately, useful) lateral movements; shoulder-in, half-pass, etc.

6

THE RIDING ARENA

Whether indoors or outdoors, the riding arena will usually be designed to double as a dressage arena, and will therefore be of set dimensions, and have standard marker letters arranged around its perimeter. These markers, together with some basic dressage movements and standard 'school' commands, will be used by the instructor to direct the ride, and it is therefore useful to be conversant with arena layout and common terminology.

▪ Dimensions

There are two sizes of arena used for dressage competitions: 60 m (197 ft) by 20 m (66 ft) and 40 m (131 ft) by 20 m (66 ft), both being rectangular. The former is used for more advanced competitions, and relatively few commercial schools possess an arena of this size; those that do may well not use it for beginners' lessons.

The smaller arena is far more common, not only because it is the appropriate size for club and local level competition, but also because it takes up less space, and is cheaper to build. For our purposes, therefore, we shall assume that this size is the 'norm'.

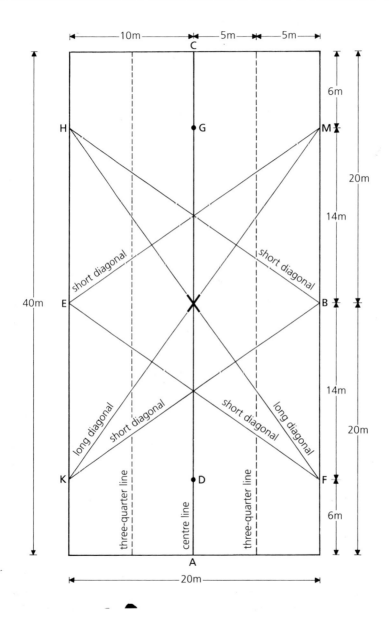

Anatomy of a 40 m (131 ft) by 20 m (66 ft) arena

■ Marker Letters (Short Arena)

These are used to establish the geography of the arena and are positioned at standard points.

Marker A is positioned halfway across one short side of the arena, and is the entry and exit point for all dressage tests. The other markers, in clockwise sequence round the perimeter, are K, E, H, C, M, B, F. This sequence can be remembered by the mnemonic 'All King Edward's Horses Can Manage Big Fences'.

Marker C is the midpoint of the other short side opposite A, and E and B represent the mid-points on the two long sides.

The other markers are known as 'quarter markers', but it is worth noting that they are *not* situated a quarter of the way down the arena from the corners (i.e. 10 m (33 ft) from the corners) but are, in fact, 6 m (20 ft) from the corners.

Whereas these markers exist physically (on boards placed around the arena), there are a further three imaginary marker points situated down the (usually imaginary) centre line (from

This pupil is working over ground poles in a fenced arena with marker letters.

A to C). These are X, the geometric centre of the arena, and D and G, which respectively represent the midpoints between K and F and H and M.

▪ Common Lines and Figures

A virtually limitless variety of lines and figures can be ridden in the arena, the only constraints being that the arena must be able to accommodate them from the chosen starting point, and that they must be physically possible for the horse to perform.

However, the lines and figures most common in teaching exercises and basic dressage use the readily identifiable markers, and/or bear a distinct relationship to the dimensions and sections of the arena. The most popular are as follows:

STRAIGHT LINES Long and short sides of the arena. Centre line AC. Three-quarter lines (halfway between centre line and long sides). Straight lines across the width of the school (EB etc.). The long diagonals (from a quarter marker to the one diagonally opposite – *not* from corner to corner). Short, or 'half-school' diagonals (from a long side midpoint to a diagonally opposite quarter marker, or vice versa). Inclines (from a marker point on the centre line to a marker on a long side, e.g. DH).

▪ Circles

In riding terminology, it is generally assumed that the dimension given for a circle represents its diameter. Any size between 20 m (66 ft) and 6 m (20 ft) diameter (the smallest a horse is generally considered able to execute correctly) can be ridden, but by far the most common sizes are 20 m (66 ft), 15 m (50 ft) and 10 m (33 ft) circles.

In addition to being technically the easiest to ride (the bigger the circle, the easier for the horse), the 20 m (66 ft) circle has

A pupil under instruction in an indoor arena.

the most obvious reference points. It can only be started from a point on a long side within 10 m (33 ft) of the mid-point marker, or from A, C, or X. If started from a point on a long side, it must, at halfway, touch the other long side opposite its starting point. If started from A or C, it must touch both long sides 10 m (33 ft) from the adjacent corners of the arena, and also pass through X. (From X, it will be the same circle but with a different starting point.)

If started from a point on a long side of the arena, 15 m (50 ft) and 10 m (33 ft) circles will touch respectively the three-quarter line and the centre line. However, since these lines are imaginary, an accurate eye and definite mental picture are needed to produce an accurate figure.

▪ Other Figures

The other figures most commonly used at novice level are mainly based upon combinations or parts of circles. They include:

FIGURE OF EIGHT This, as the name suggests, consists of one circle followed immediately by a second circle of the same size ridden in the opposite direction. The easiest and most common figure of eight consists of two 'back-to-back' 20 m (66 ft) circles starting from X. These should be ridden accurately; the figure should not be allowed to degenerate into a vague curve at each end of the school, interspersed by wavering trips along the long diagonals.

HALF CIRCLES These are often incorporated into movements for changing direction, for example a half 10 m (33 ft) circle from E to X, followed by an incline back to the long side at K, or a half 10 m (33 ft) circle from B to X, followed by another half circle from X to E.

It should be noted that a half circle is commenced in the same manner as a full circle from the same point. For instance, a 20 m (66 ft) circle from E touches the long sides of the arena at E and B, with the line EB being its diameter. Therefore, half a 20 m (66 ft) circle from E is the first half of this circle and not (as sometimes attempted) a loop from E back to the corner of the arena – a movement which is physically impossible for the horse to perform correctly.

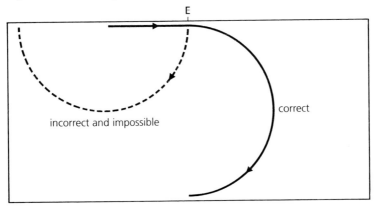

Half circle from a given point

SERPENTINES A serpentine is a series of half circles or arcs (commonly described as 'loops') of equal size, curving in alternate directions. The size and depth of the loops can be varied, and the figure is sometimes extended (and made easier to ride) by the inclusion of short straight sections between loops. This, in fact, is the case with the most commonly ridden serpentine of three loops from side to side, and the full length, of the arena (three half circles of approximately 13 m (43 ft) diameter, interspersed with straight lines a couple of strides long).

SHALLOW LOOPS Shallow loops can be of various sizes, but are essentially arcs of large circles ridden 'against' the general direction of travel. For instance, if a rider is proceeding 'right-handed' round the arena perimeter, and rides a shallow loop from 'K' to 'H', this should take the form of a symmetrical 'left-handed' curve passing through a point a few metres (3–5 m) to the 'inside' of 'E'.

These figures are ridden initially as exercises in general control and maintenance of correct 'bend' in the horse, and later as an introduction to movements such as counter-canter.

Schoolfigures are not simply ends in themselves, or even just exercises in rider control. Performed correctly, they have the positive functions of making the horse more supple and athletic. However, if the horse is allowed to wander about and avoid working properly, he will not derive benefit from the exercises.

OPPOSITE PAGE Some examples of common school movements. Diagrams of circles are merely examples of points from which the circles may be ridden; they are not intended to show sequential movements. For example, 15 m (50 ft) circle: these overlap on diagram because they would do so in fact.

The purpose of the illustration is to show a selection of the movements which a rider may be asked to perform between the stages of beginner and 'club competitor'.

The most unusual movement illustrated is the four-loop serpentine, which is included to show a variation from the ubiquitous three-loop figure and to provide an example of a correct figure ridden about the centre line.

■ Non-standard Arenas

It should be noted that, in some instances, an arena may not conform to the normal dimensions. This can create confusion between instructor and pupils if terminology relating to the

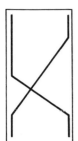

changing rein
across long and
short diagonals

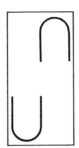

turns to or from
centre line

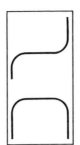

turns across
school changing
or maintaining
rein

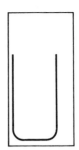

turn onto or
from three-
quarter line

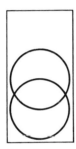

20m circles

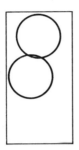

15m circles

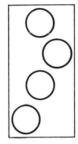

10m circles

two half 10m
circles to
change rein

half 10m circle
inclining back
to outside track

three loop
serpentine to
cover whole
arena

serpentine of
half 10m
circles about
centre line

shallow loop
down long side

These pupils are 'going large' – a cone has been strategically placed to ensure they don't cut across the corner.

standard arena is loosely applied. If, for instance, in an arena 25 m (82 ft) wide, the instruction is given to ride a 20 m (66 ft) circle, what the instructor *probably* means is 'ride a circle whose diameter is the width of the school'.

While such inconsistencies are not crucially important within the framework of an ordinary lesson, it is, nevertheless, helpful if instructions can be defined at the outset. Such arenas are, however, obviously unsuitable for anything approaching formal competitive dressage.

▪ Terms and Commands

In addition to using the marker letters and their intersecting lines in giving commands ('diagonally across the arena from K to M', etc.), the instructor will also use common terms relating to the arena itself. Some of these will also relate to where, to whom, and/or how they are used. Let us look at some. Relating to the arena, the most common are:

THE OUTSIDE TRACK The widest practical route around the perimeter of the arena.

THE INSIDE TRACK A route parallel to, but a metre or so inside, the outside track. (Used for practising turns, passing the rest of the 'ride', etc.)

GO LARGE Proceed around the outside track.

THE INSIDE (leg, rein, etc.) That on the concave side of any bend in the horse; when the horse is straight, that nearer the centre of the arena.

THE OUTSIDE The opposite of the inside.

ON THE LEFT REIN Going anti-clockwise.

ON THE RIGHT REIN Going clockwise.

CHANGE THE REIN An adjunct to a command to perform a movement which will result in going in the opposite direction to before.

Commands relating to a class of pupils include:

FORM A RIDE Proceed (usually) round the outside track in single file, normally with one horse's length between the horses.

THE WHOLE RIDE Everyone together.

LEADING FILE The rider in front of the established 'ride'.

REAR FILE The rider at the rear of the established 'ride'.

OPEN ORDER At an early stage, this usually means that horses are spread fairly evenly around the perimeter of the arena 'on the same rein', rather than working 'as a ride'. At a more advanced level, 'work in open order' may signify that riders can change direction and gait according to their wishes. This obviously calls for common sense, discretion and alertness. Should two riders converge from opposite directions, the rule is to pass 'left shoulder to left shoulder'.

In addition, there is an old command of military origin 'make much of your horses'. Given at the end of a lesson, it means simply allow the horse a long rein (so that he can stretch his neck) and give him a pat. Not only does this relate directly to the 'correction and reward' system of training a horse, it also serves as a useful reminder that one is not astride a mechanical object.

This arena has been divided so that several lessons can proceed at the same time.

7

OTHER ASPECTS OF LEARNING

▪ Lunge lessons

Lungeing involves a trainer/instructor working a horse on a circle, using a lunge line, lungeing whip and his voice as means of control. The lunge line is attached to the horse's head by means of a lungeing cavesson – a special headcollar which can be fitted instead of, or in addition to, the bridle. There are various reasons for lungeing a horse, but the one which concerns us is that it can be a valuable means of instructing a pupil – if done correctly.

The principle of a lunge lesson is that the instructor initially takes full control of the horse (the pupil not holding the reins, which are secured out of harm's way), and the rider is free to concentrate upon improving his posture and depth of seat, and absorbing the 'feel' of the horse at various gaits. At a later stage, he may also study the applications of 'seat and back' aids.

The basic requirements for any good riding lesson – safe environment, suitable horse, experienced teacher and a balanced and progressive programme – become more crucial where lunge lessons are concerned. Given such conditions, these lessons can be of great value, and should accelerate the learning process. However, if any of these conditions are not met, more harm than good may result. Lunge lessons should, therefore, be taken with discretion, at centres where they form a regular and established part of the teaching process, and not at yards where the 'lunge-ing arena' is a field full of loose horses, or where the staff have to 'see if we've got a horse who will lunge'.

Because of the intensity of lunge lessons, they should not greatly exceed 20 minutes' duration – especially in the earlier stages.

▪ Riding Out

In the early pages of this book, I was at pains to persuade the reader to have greater ambition than merely to go out for what amounts to the occasional mounted stroll. This does not, of course, mean that riding out should not be enjoyable in itself as well as forming part of the learning process. However, any rider who is keen to progress should look upon riding out as an oppor-tunity both to put what he has already learnt into practice, and to broaden his experience.

Once pupils have reached a level of basic competence in the arena, it is usual for most riding schools to offer the chance to venture outdoors. These rides should, of course, be escorted by at least one experienced adult member of staff (two, if there are more than a handful of riders and/or it is necessary to ride on public roads). They should also take place in as safe as environ-ment as possible and pupils should, whenever practical, be mounted on horses who they have a proven ability to control.

However, even if these criteria are all adhered to, the novice will find that riding out is, in many ways, a new experience. The open spaces, natural environment and change of regime will make most horses keener and livelier than they are in the arena (the less often they go out, the greater the probable difference), and there will be attractions and distractions which are absent from the arena. Furthermore, the environment will be different for the rider, who is likely to experience for the first time riding on varied terrain and ground conditions, and the possible haz-

When riding out the rider may experience unexpected hazards.

ards of overhanging branches, knee-savaging gate posts, road-works, loose dogs, lost joggers and the other paraphernalia of the countryside.

In order to cope with these delights and distractions, there are several general points the rider should bear in mind:

1. Listen to, and obey, any commands/requests of the escort(s) promptly. The escort will (or should) be familiar with the locality and used to perceiving and coping with hazards and situations which may not be apparent to the inexperienced rider.

2. The stirrups should be shortened a little. We have already discussed the need to shorten the stirrups before riding at gallop/strong canter. While this should not take place on the rider's first few ventures out of doors, it still makes sense to shorten the leathers a hole or two from 'school' length.

Uneven terrain, varying ground conditions and the general demands of riding out in a group increase the chances of 'losing' a stirrup if there is any tendency to be 'reaching' for them, and the rider will have enough to think about without 'fishing' for stirrups or riding 'one-sided'.

3. Prepare mentally for the possible changes in the horse's attitude. In addition to a general increase in keenness, his natural instincts will come to the fore, and he will be likely to try to snatch mouthfuls of anything that takes his fancy, and be more concerned with the antics of the 'herd' than the wishes of his rider. If he is familiar with the route, he may also tend to change gait automatically at places where he expects to trot, canter, rest, etc.

Riding out makes most horses keener and livelier than they are in the arena.

In order to avoid becoming a 'passenger' it may be necessary to ride more firmly and positively than when in the school; while the principles of equitation should not be abandoned, the rider should be more concerned with effectiveness than with the ultimate niceties. The horse should not be allowed to eat (it is not only 'bad manners' – there are several common plants which are poisonous to horses), and the rider should ensure that he continues to give effective aids, and does not just allow the horse to do what the others are doing of his own accord.

It is worth noting that success in these matters will not only improve the rider's effectiveness when riding out, it will also enhance his confidence and make him more demanding of himself and the horse when in the school.

In addition to these general points, there are some more specific areas in which it is necessary to combine commonsense with riding skills in the interests of safety.

▪ **Roadsense**

In many areas nowadays, it is impossible to reach open land without riding on public roads – although this should, in the early stages, be kept to a practical minimum. While it is the responsibility of the escort(s) to ensure the safety of the ride, the riders also have a responsibility to act in a manner which makes this task as easy as possible. Also, in the last resort, the individual has responsibility for any action he instigates, and it is only the rider who can have direct control over his horse. Riders should, therefore:

1. Ride with care, attention, and to the best of their ability.

2. Pay extra attention to the commands of the escort and, in particular, keep to their allotted position and at their allotted distances (straggling, especially, can cause serious problems and provoke dangerous situations).

3. Draw prompt attention to any untoward incident which affects their ability to carry out the above.

4. Acknowledge any courtesy shown by other road users; this is constructive as well as polite.

It is in the interests of all riders who use the roads (whether escorted or not) to be familiar with the requirements of the Highway Code as they apply to general road users, as well as with the sections relating specifically to those riding/leading horses. The British Horse Society's Riding And Road Safety Test (usually organised by clubs affiliated to the B.H.S.) gives an excellent grounding in the principles of riding safely on public roads, and may prove instructive and thought-provoking even for the more experienced rider. (Useful background literature is obtainable direct from the B.H.S.)

▪ Shying

Shying is an instinctive reaction which takes the form of the horse jumping sideways away from a source of sudden fright. While some highly-strung horses will shy at the slightest disturbance, and some will 'look for things to shy at' out of mischief or over-freshness, these characteristics should not be apparent in horses provided for inexperienced riders. Nevertheless, any horse may shy if he is genuinely startled and, in a group of horses, the actions of one may spark off similar reactions in others. It is useful, therefore, if riders are aware of the causes of shying, and understand how to avoid the problem whenever possible and how to cope with incipient shying should it occur.

Since the problem is usually most dangerous if it occurs on the road, the following points should be considered in conjunction with those made above:

1. Well-trained horses of good temperament, who are familiar with the normal sights and sounds of their environment, will usually only shy if genuinely frightened by the very sudden manifestation of a very strange sight or sound. The problem here is that the horse is likely to become aware of the object that frightens him at the same time, or before, the rider. In

---

Many horses are suspicious of drains and manhole covers. This can be a result of their smell, but they are also slippery to walk on. Where traffic conditions make it safe to do so, avoid riding directly over these objects – especially in trot.

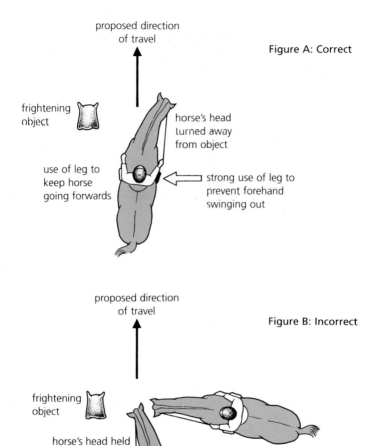

proposed direction
of travel

Figure A: Correct

frightening
object

horse's head
turned away
from object

use of leg to
keep horse
going forwards

strong use of leg to
prevent forehand
swinging out

proposed direction
of travel

Figure B: Incorrect

frightening
object

horse's head held
towards object

leg aids push
horse towards
object

quarters swing out
so that horse is
facing object and
blocking way

Dealing with shying

such circumstances, the shying may well occur before the rider is able to prevent it, and he can do little except rely on a secure seat and bring the horse under control as quickly as possible. Although this type of shying can obviously be potentially dangerous (and is a reason why other road users should always give horses plenty of room), the 'genuine' horse shying for a 'genuine' reason is unlikely to make a meal of it, and will quickly calm down if the rider himself remains calm and sympathetic.

2. Notwithstanding the above, it is obviously preferable if the rider *can* foresee the problem and circumvent it. While he should not become a nervous wreck, imagining dangers at every step, he should be constantly alert to anything which might frighten the horse. Although the list is not exhaustive, common things to be aware of include: noisy/unusual road traffic, roadworks and building sites adjacent to roads, anything shiny or flapping by the roadside (refuse sacks, flags, flashing lights, etc.), pedestrians with umbrellas, loose dogs, noisy gardening machinery and lawn sprinklers in operation. These items will not *necessarily* cause a horse to shy but, if the rider believes that any object might cause concern, he should take the following precautions:

   i. He should *not* tense up himself. Tension will only transfer itself to the horse at a time when he needs reassurance.
   ii. If on a road, he should check the situation with regard to other traffic. If he is likely to converge upon the suspect object at the same time as other road users he should, wherever practical, halt at a safe place a sensible distance from the object until the way is clear.
   iii. When safe to do so, he should take as wide a route as possible round the object, turning the horse's head a little away from it, and riding him well forward between leg and hand, whilst encouraging him with the voice.

A quiet lane is ideal for the first experience of riding out.

3. If the rider senses that the horse is seriously worried by the object and/or circumstances force him to pass close to it, he should turn the horse's head definitely away from it, and apply both legs firmly. The leg on the side away from the object should be applied very firmly indeed, and slightly further forward than usual. In a truly dangerous situation, this leg has *got* to prevent the horse turning his forehand outwards, and the rider should be prepared to apply it as strongly as he is capable of.

It should be noted that trying to 'hold the horse straight' by pulling on the rein nearer the object is a serious mistake. As with riding a circle, it will just encourage the horse to swing his quarters out, and he may end up facing the object which is frightening him. In such a position, he will be side on to the intended direction of travel, he will be virtually blocking a narrow road and, in order to get further from the source of his fear his most direct route will be *backwards*.

Regarding going backwards, the horse who shows a tendency to whip round and run away from the source of his fear should, wherever possible, be prevented from doing so, and driven forwards past it. While it is preferable for a horse to pass frightening objects as calmly as possible, hurrying *past* them is much better than running away from them, and allowing the latter course of action sets a dangerous precedent, and stores up trouble for the future.

Finally on the subject, while firm handling may be necessary to deal with a shying horse, punishment is inappropriate unless the rider is absolutely convinced that the action is contrived. Even then, considerable discretion is called for; the rider must have regard to the practicalities of the situation and, more importantly, he must ask *why* the horse is behaving in such a way.

▪ Canter and Gallop in a 'Ride'

Once riders are used to controlling their horses in the open at the slower gaits, they will be given the opportunity to have their first outdoor canter. Any sensible escort will ensure that this takes place on good going, along a reasonably open route, preferably somewhat uphill and not directly towards 'home'. It is also helpful if there is a safe and definite stopping point at the end of the proposed route.

At such an early stage, riders should definitely not be encouraged to gallop but, when they become sufficiently experienced to do so, the following points concerning canter should be considered even more crucial at the faster gait.

1. Initially, riders will probably be instructed to canter in single file, possibly being sent off one at a time. While there are good reasons for doing this, it is likely that those horses 'waiting their turn' will become eager and restless, and riders may find it quite testing to retain control. In order to cope with such a situation, the rider should sit erect, keep his legs gently 'on' the horse, and push him into a 'containing' rein contact. In other words, he should adhere to the correct principles of equitation, and not be tempted to take his legs away from the horse's side and/or snatch at the reins.

Most importantly, he should keep the horse facing more or less in the direction of those departing. The popular idea that the horse will calm down if turned away from the departing 'herd' is quite erroneous; such action is much more likely to excite/upset him further. I have known of a rider sustaining serious injury when their horse slipped and fell whilst whipping round after being turned away from the departing ride; it is not a practice I would recommend.

2. When the turn comes to canter, the horse should be given a proper aid, and ridden up into the rein contact, so that the required gait and speed are established. The rider who just 'turns the horse loose' with a whoop of delight or shriek of terror, is likely to get what he is asking for ('carted'). It is, in fact, sensible to start off a little slower than is strictly necessary, then, once the horse has 'settled' he can be asked to 'go on' a little more, and the posture adapted accordingly. The horse must, however, be allowed sufficiently forward to canter in comfort – 'hanging on' grimly will confuse and upset him and probably *provoke* him into fighting for his head and going crooked.

3. When cantering in single file, riders should endeavour to keep their distances. In the interests of those following, a rider on a sluggish horse should try to push him on, but the chief onus of avoiding trouble rests on the rider behind. He should, therefore, maintain sufficient control to prevent his

Reflective clothing for horse and rider is necessary at night and in conditions of poor visibilty.

horse 'running up the backside' of the horse in front. Although getting directly behind another horse may assist in restraining one's own mount, it can also provoke the leading horse into kicking out, or result in the horse behind 'clipping his heels', either of which can cause a serious accident.

4. By the same token, where inexperienced riders are involved, horses should not be allowed to overtake others, since this can result in 'racing' or even (if there is an outstanding 'herd hierarchy' dispute) an inter-horse 'punch up'. At a later stage, when all riders are experienced and aware of the characters of the horses, overtaking may be permissible but *only* when there is plenty of room, and subject to specific agreement from the rider in front. Even then, considerable care should be exercised; shouting 'coming past' and then putting the other rider into the brambles will not increase one's popularity.

5. Even more common sense and courtesy will be required when riders are sufficiently experienced to canter/gallop in a group.

*Riders should not
be allowed to overtake*

In addition to being able to control speed to a fine degree, riders must also be fully capable of controlling direction, keeping horses straight or manoeuvring as required to avoid bumping or squeezing others, and to avoid such trouble themselves. However skilful the riders, horses of unknown/uncertain temperament should always be kept on the outside of the group.

■ Jumping

This book is written as an introduction to riding 'on the flat' and, since jumping is a branch of equitation which follows on from this, it is not my intention to discuss it here in any detail. This is not to imply that jumping, undertaken in due season, is a particularly difficult or awesome business; in fact, the ability to ride over jumps will open up a whole new spectrum of activity,

The rider needs to achieve competence on the flat before learning to jump.

and I would heartily encourage readers to explore this field at an appropriate stage.

However, there are good reasons why jumping should not be attempted too early in a rider's career:

1. Jumping correctly and safely requires of the rider a greater degree of balance and 'independence' of seat than one might 'get away with' on the flat.

2. Although jumping a course of fences consists largely of riding 'on the flat' between them, this riding must be of good standard if the horse is to be presented at the obstacles in such a way that he can readily negotiate them.

It is, therefore, futile and potentially dangerous to start jumping too soon, and my main purpose in broaching the topic is to warn against doing so, lest an activity which should prove enjoyable and exhilarating be abandoned after premature false starts and possible accident. There is, in my opinion, a tendency for some schools to introduce jumping before pupils are ready for it, and there are certainly enthusiastic riders who want to 'have a go' before they are capable of doing so successfully. While enthusiasm for progress is an admirable trait, it needs to be tempered by sound instruction and a realistic assessment of ability.

Unfortunately, observation suggests that the general standard of jumping tuition is somewhat lower than the general standard of tuition in flatwork, and that instruction is too frequently given by people whose practical experience is alarmingly limited, forcing them to rely upon hazy and sometimes unrealistic theory. The common result of combining pupils who are 'not ready' with instructors of this sort is that the instructor will realise that a pupil is interfering, or likely to interfere with his horse's efforts but, instead of adjourning attempts at jumping pending further riding experience, he may encourage the pupil to perform movements or adopt postures which the teacher thinks will assist the horse but which will, almost certainly, place the rider in a highly precarious position. The consequence is an introduction to jumping which consists of falls, refusals and rider confusion – and does little for the horse's training or enthusiasm.

This unfortunate state of affairs can be avoided (at least in part) by ensuring that pupils are reasonably proficient riders before they commence jumping. While it is not easy to make hard-and-fast rules about what constitutes 'ready to jump', I would suggest that the rider should certainly be capable of exercising a fair degree of control in canter (as opposed to merely being able to canter round the arena without falling off!).

The reader who wishes to explore the basic issues of jumping theory and technique may find another book in this series, *Riding Over Jumps*, of interest.

CONCLUSION

It is my hope that the ideas and principles outlined in this book will assist readers in the early stage of their riding careers, and encourage them to ride in a thoughtful and enquiring manner. However, I would like to conclude by re-emphasising the desirability of continual progress, especially since I am well aware of the constraints which apply to many riders.

I have noticed over a number of years that the vast majority of people who are reasonably keen riders can and do reach a 'basic competence' level but then, in many cases, the rate of improvement slows, or virtually stops, often counter to the rider's real wishes. This is a great pity, especially since such riders are reaching a stage from which they could go on to better things. I feel that there are three main reasons for this this 'tailing off'; complacency, lack of belief and lack of opportunity.

■ Complacency

This may arise because the rider knows that he can ride the basic movements and gaits on a well-mannered horse (even though he may not do so particularly well) and feels that there is little more to learn. Difficulties encountered tend to be blamed on the

There is a lot to be gained from the companionship of a horse.

horse, and such a rider will show little inclination to tackle a less straightforward mount, even one of considerable ability. This attitude is, of course, the rider's own business, and if he is genuinely content to remain at such a standard then there is little more to be said. Very often, however, such an attitude will go hand-in-glove with the 'if only I had a better horse' syndrome, indicating that the complacency is really false, and that the rider does want to achieve more, but is looking everywhere except to his own ability.

To anyone who finds themselves thinking along such lines, I would suggest firstly that they make an honest assessment of how the horses they usually ride perform for other people; this may provide a truer perspective of their actual ability. Secondly, I would suggest that they resolve to try and ride each horse they sit on a little better in all respects than they have ever done before. Learning to ride is not a matter of smooth progression; it is best equated to stumbling erratically up an uneven and endless flight of stairs. From any current standpoint, it may be difficult to see that there *is* another stair (let alone how to get to it), but the progress of continually seeking improvement can result in sudden and dramatic progress, and should certainly banish destructively complacent thoughts. It is no coincidence that the very best riders tend to be the most (constructively) self-critical of all.

Lack of Belief

This is pretty much the opposite of complacency, and may be exhibited by the thoughtful rider who realises early on how little he knows, and perhaps compares his own abilities with those of famous riders (or even his instructor) and concludes that he will never be able to 'ride like that'. While, as we have just seen, realistic self-appraisal is very healthy, it should not be allowed to degenerate into self-degradation and the abandonment of all ambition. Although very few riders are every going to achieve top-level success, there is no reason why everyone else should not ride as though they were trying to, and there is no reason why anyone who is able to ride regularly should not reach a standard at which they can perform respectably at club and local shows, and dismount from the average horse leaving him going a little better than when they got on.

The inevitable setbacks and disappointments encountered in riding should not, therefore, be thought of as overwhelming proof of failure, but as lessons from which to learn. While comparisons of riding ability may be instructive, the rider who sees the horse he has been riding going much better for someone else should not think of this solely in terms of his own incompetence and the other rider's skill, but rather as evidence of the horse's capability. Once aware of this, he will be better placed to concentrate his efforts towards achieving similar results.

Lack of Opportunity

The most stifling and frustrating cause of rider stagnation, this tends to affect especially those riders who are short of time and

There is no reason why anyone who rides regularly should not reach show standard.

money. There are numerous riding schools which, for various reasons, are unable or unwilling to offer tuition beyond the basics and many riders feel, after a while, that they are fed up with doing the same thing week after week. Even though there may be scope for improving the things they are doing, such stale repetition is bound to dull incentive, and keen riders in such a position have got to take steps to change matters before they are driven to abandon riding in favour of stamp collecting.

The most obvious step in such circumstances is to find another school which offers greater scope for improvement. Such an establishment is likely to be less accessible (otherwise it would, presumably, already be the chosen school), and this may mean riding less frequently. However, there is no doubt that the keen rider of average ability will benefit more from fortnightly lessons from a good instructor who respects his desire to improve, than from weekly visits to an establishment which looks upon him primarily as a source of income.

Furthermore, this type of establishment is more likely to be sympathetic towards requests to hire a horse for participation in local riding club events, and this is a course which the keen rider

There is a big world beyond the walls of the riding school!

would do well to pursue. Not only can it add a new dimension to his riding, and get him out of the confines of the riding school, it may also prove fruitful in terms of new friendships and contacts. It is surprising how many people are looking for someone to share or help exercise a horse, and the right arrangement at the right time can put riding into a whole new perspective. For any contemplating ownership at a future stage, this sort of experience can prove invaluable.

Obviously, so far as this sort of opportunity is concerned, the more proficient the rider becomes, the more avenues are likely to open. This is one good reason why the frustrated rider should not give up or give in, but keep trying to improve regardless of current constraints. There is a big world beyond the walls of the riding school, and it contains more able horses than able riders. Why not help redress the balance?